ULTIMATE OLIVE OIL

For Healthy Living

JENNY STACEY

Published in 2001 by Caxton Editions
20 Bloomsbury Street
London WC1B 3JH
a member of the Caxton Publishing Group

© 2001 Caxton Publishing Group

Designed and produced for Caxton Editions
by Open Door Limited
Langham, Rutland

Editing: Alison Leach, Mary Morton
Setting and layout: Richard Booth
Digital imagery © copyright PhotoDisc Inc.
Film production: GA Graphics, Stamford, UK

Title: Ultimate Olive Oil
ISBN: 1-84067 356 7

Printed and bound by CTPS

ULTIMATE OLIVE OIL

For Healthy Living

JENNY STACEY

CAXTON EDITIONS

CONTENTS

6 INTRODUCTION

The History of Olive Oil

The olive tree and olive oil date way back in history. Over the centuries, varied uses have been made of both the branches and the fruit. Indeed, the olive and its production has come a long way since the planting of the first tree.

The olive tree first grew wild in the Middle East and olives have been used for various purposes since prehistoric times: no one knows who first pressed the olive to obtain the oil. Homer referred to olive oil as liquid gold and in ancient Greece it was rubbed over the bodies of athletes as a ritual before competitions. Owing to its importance as a source of food and light, olive oil has gained a religious and divine significance. Drops of oil were poured into the tombs of dead saints and martyrs through small holes. Being symbols of benediction and purification, olive trees were also offered to deities and powerful figures – some were even found in Tutankhamen's tomb.

Olive oil has been more than just a food for the people of the Mediterranean, being also used for medicinal purposes. Considered to be magical, it was an endless source of fascination, known as the fountain of great wealth and power.

One of the earliest references to the olive occurs in an ancient Egyptian papyrus from the 12th century BC: it is a deed of gift to the god Ra from the Pharaoh Ramses III, who offered the olives from the groves planted around Heliopolis as a fuel for light. Legend states that an olive tree grew along with a cypress and a cedar on Adam's grave on the slopes of Mount Tabor.

There are also numerous references to the olive in the Bible. The olive tree was, and still remains, a symbol of abundance, glory and peace, and its leafy branches were used to crown the victorious in both games and war. The Bible tells us that the dove brought an olive branch back to Noah in the Ark, which proved that the floods were subsiding, and ever since then the olive branch has been a symbol of

peace and goodwill. In the land of the Hebrews, King Solomon and King David placed great importance on the cultivation of olive groves and even appointed guards to protect the trees.

Olive trees dominated Greece and were regarded as sacred in Hellenic society. Indeed, if a person cut a tree down, this was punishable by death. In ancient Greece and Rome the olive was the hottest commodity, and special ships were built to transport them from Greece around the Mediterranean. The belief that olive oil conferred strength and youth was widespread. In ancient Egypt, Greece and Rome it was infused with flowers and grasses to make medicine, and the oil has anointed the noblest of heads throughout history.

Olive culture has ancient roots: fossilized remains of the ancestors of the olive tree were found near Livorno in Italy and these date back 20 million years. That said, cultivation probably didn't occur there until the 5th century BC. The first olives are thought to have been cultivated in the Eastern Mediterranean region known as 'the fertile crescent', from where they gradually moved westwards over the years.

Greek mythology tells us that Zeus promised to give Attica to the god or goddess who showed him the most useful invention and it was Athene, the goddess of wisdom and peace who won by offering the olive tree with its nourishing oil. Athene became the goddess of Athens and her olive tree was said to have been planted on the rock of the Acropolis. The tree that stands there today is thought to have grown from a shoot of the original tree.

Over several millennia, 14000–5000 BC, olive cultivation spread from Crete to Syria, Palestine and Israel and on to southern Turkey, Cyprus and Egypt, until in 5000 BC it reached Greece; Mycenae in particular cultivated the olive. With the expansion of the Greek colonies, it reached southern Italy and North Africa in the 8th century BC and then spread to southern France, Spain and Portugal. Olive trees were eventually planted in all of the Mediterranean region under Roman rule, and it was the Romans who invented the screw press to extract the oil and who also improved the storage of the oil. Olive trees were cultivated in Provence in France, though less oil was reaped from these trees than elsewhere. Spain was one of the better producers of oil and clay pots from Spain have been dug up in Italy which bear the mark of an exporter, showing that trends have not changed greatly and that, even then, Spain was producing larger quantities of oil.

The trade of oil halted with the end of the Roman Empire, but the olive tree was well established and survived, again becoming important in the Middle Ages, when oil was required to light the lamps in churches during this time of monastic dominance. In the 13th century, Italian monks in Apulia began widespread olive cultivation and laid the foundations for the vast oil industry in Italy today, along with Florence, which became a great market for olive oil, and has remained so despite decreased production in the Tuscan area today. Special flat-bottomed boats were built in Venice to transport the jars of olive oil that were produced in southern Italy, back to northern Italy, which was more densely populated. In the 14th century, the first regulatory board, the 'Visdomini di Tenaria', was set up to control the import and export of olive oil. The trade was so important to

southern Italy that after the Spanish conquest, when the area was taken, a road was built, linking Apulia to Naples for rapid transportation of the oil.

For centuries, oil production was run as family businesses, and then co-operatives began to form in some areas, until the end of the 19th century when industrial oil-refining plants were developed. Some small production centres remained in each producing country, producing the finer extra-virgin oils or simply meeting local demand, but the majority of oil was shipped to the refinery, where it was mixed and pressed before being shipped around the world. This mass production might have continued were it not for the fact that scientists in America began to realize the nutritional advantages of oil. This coincided with a trend for quality produced foodstuffs, from smaller suppliers, which has led to a revival of quality oils. Olives are now grown all around the world where there is a suitable climate, being cultivated in California, Australia, Mexico, Argentina, South Africa and New Zealand, to name but a few.

The Growing of Olives

Cultivated olives belong to a group known as *sativa*, the wild olives being known as *oleaster*. They both grow readily in a Mediterranean climate or similar, preferring hot, dry summers and cool winters. Although sensitive to cold, they require a cooler period to remain dormant and rest when not growing. They are able to withstand freezing temperatures for short periods of time as long as the temperature does not fall below 10°C/50°F, when they will die. Although they will not produce such a good harvest, they can withstand long periods without rain. According to Italian folklore, sun, stone, drought, silence and solitude are the five main ingredients required to create ideal conditions for the olive tree. The majority of the world's olive trees grow in the Mediterranean countries, but they are also grown in the southern hemisphere under similar climatic conditions.

Vines and olives are often grown side by side as they require the same conditions, the olives being used as windbreaks for the vines. Olive trees can grow on poor, stony ground and at high or low altitudes, which is unsuitable for any other crops, making them a popular and lucrative crop in areas that would otherwise be unused.

The trees take five years to yield their first olives and another 10 to 15 years to reach their full capacity. However, once established, they will live for many years, some even surviving for over a hundred years.

The unripe fruit of the olive tree is green and pear-shaped, changing to a dark purple colour or black as they ripen. All olives left on a tree will follow this ripening pattern. Green olives are, therefore, unripe olives, and black olives those that have been left to complete the pattern. Those that are to be pressed for oil can be picked at any stage, but if unripe they will generally produce a bitter-flavoured oil, and yield will be reduced.

Types of Olive

There are over 50 types of olives, each one very distinctive in flavour and each suitable for a different purpose. The Spanish Picaul is very suited to oil production, whereas the French Lucque is a better table olive. The Italian Franoio produces a hot oil whilst the Italian Taggiasca gives a sweeter-tasting oil. Some olives are native to a specific area and cannot be grown outside it, and oils are often produced from a mixture of these. Other growers cultivate the crop differently and plant different areas of their land with different varieties of olives, and press and bottle them individually.

During its life, the pruning, harvesting and growing conditions of the olive tree all have a bearing on the resultant fruit and its quality, and many areas therefore have traditional 'farming' methods to suit the region.

Getting the harvest right is extremely crucial to the yield and quality of the final oil. All growers want optimum yield, which means the fruits must be as ripe as possible, but if the olives are left to ripen for too long they will oxidize once picked and the oil will be poor. Newly harvested olives are quite easily damaged, so care must be taken when harvesting. In some of the smaller areas, they are still harvested by hand using rakes to 'comb' the trees. Nets are suspended above the ground to catch the olives as they fall. In poorer areas, nets are suspended and nature is left to take its course, the olives falling naturally and the nets being emptied as required. This can lead to poor oils being produced. In cooler climates, this is not so much of a problem, as the olives are allowed to warm a little so that they produce more oil.

Italy

Italy is one of the top oil-producing countries (in competition with Spain), its hilly countryside and climate being ideal for olive trees. There is only one region of Italy that does not produce oil: the Val d'Aosta in northern Italy. Tuscany, on the other hand, has built up a reputation for excellent olive oil and produces more extra-virgin oil than any other region. Oils from Lake Garda and Liguria in the north are beginning to become popular, but it is still the southern part of the country that produces the most oil. Calabria and Apulia produce 70% of Italy's oil, followed by 11% from Sicily and 5% from Campania. Oils from all of these areas are blended and sold under brand names, but there is a trend developing for growers to produce their own, high-quality oils and sell them under their own names. This is perhaps due to the high profile given recently to the 'Mediterranean-style' diet and its health benefits by the media around the world.

Despite producing fine oils, Italy also imports olive oil for processing, which means that not all oils exported from Italy are Italian in origin.

Italy has several native varieties of olive, the most important of these being the Coratina from the south; Frantoio, Leccino, and Moraiolo from the central regions; and Taggiasca from the north.

Spain

Olive trees are found in every region of Spain, it being one of the world's largest producers. As it is so hot and dry, the harvests are terrific, and the olives are harvested both as table olives and for oil production. Jaen and Cordoba produce a large proportion of Spain's harvest, and most olives are grown by small farmers and taken to factories or a large co-operative for pressing. In some areas, such as Baena and Sierra de Segura, there are single estates producing their own high-quality oils. Many different varieties of olive are grown in Spain as well, the most important of these being Arbequina and Verdial, Picudo and Picaul, Hojiblanca and Lechin.

In terms of harvesting, the olives are usually hand-picked and then pressed in hydraulic or centrifugal presses. As the Spanish are now making a concerted effort to reduce the time between harvesting and pressing, Spain is producing finer oils, particularly where table oils are concerned, the Manzanillo and Gordal olives being the main varieties used.

Greece

Greece is the third largest producer of olive oil, and one of the highest consumers. Trees are traditionally grown in the mountainous region in the west of the country, where there are mainly small farms, each producing around 400 kg/880 lb. The olives are taken to co-operatives, where they are mixed and sold as blends. There is a growing trend for groves to be planted in the central region of the country, as well as on the Greek islands. Crete has a long tradition of olive oil production, as does the island of Lesbos, both supplying to the mainland. Greek oil has only recently been marketed as a premium product. Previously, the best oils were exported to Italy, and there are few single-estate oils (unlike Spain), but the oil is of good quality and not inferior as many would believe.

The Greek olive most of us know is the Kalamata. Although it has a good flavour, it is not generally used for oil production, but is produced as a table olive. One of the best oil-producing olives is the Koroneiki, grown in the Kalamata area, which causes much confusion. Mani is the rival oil-producing area.

France

France produces very high standard oils and table olives, due to its climate, and the majority of the growing areas are along the Mediterranean coast, stretching from the Spanish border to the Italian Riviera. It remains one of the smaller producers, despite its high-quality products. One of the main areas of production for oil is Nyons in Provence; other important areas being Vallée des Baux, Vaucluse, Gard and Alpes Maritimes. France has only a small number of varieties growing, most of which are used for both oil and table olive production; the main varieties are La Tanche, Picholine, Grossane, Salonenque, Lucque and Cailletier.

United States

California is the main producer of olives in the USA, although Oregon, Washington State and Texas are also producers. Until recently, the Americans have concentrated on producing table olives but, with the heightened interest in the health benefits of olive oil, they are now producing oils as well. The most common olive grown is the Mission, then the Manzanillo and Sevillano, all of which produce good-quality oils. It is only since the late 1980s that a group of farmers have taken a new approach to oil production and have planted new groves that will produce oils of a quality able to compete with the European varieties. Most are using Italian varieties of olive and, in the near future, they will produce larger quantities and better quality oils.

Other Areas of Production

Portugal has many olive trees, but the countryside is so barren that the yield is quite low and the quality not as high as in other countries. There is less importance placed on the olive harvest and oil production and the climate is not as suitable as in other countries. Most of the oil produced in Portugal is consumed in the home and not sold commercially.

Tunisia, surprisingly, is the next largest producer of olive oil after Spain, Italy and Greece and the largest producer in North Africa. Oil production is a major employer in the country and is therefore very important. It largely exports oil to non-European countries. Morocco and Algeria, the Middle East, Libya and Argentina all produce oil, accounting for around 7% of the world market.

Other countries that produce oil are Australia, New Zealand and South Africa, but at present their production is very small. This may change, as it has in America, with the increasing popularity of olive oil.

Olive oils are distinguished and classified by category, from pure to extra-virgin, this being determined by the acidity of the oil. The traditional methods of harvesting and production have not changed greatly since they first began, but the equipment used has become more sophisticated. The olives are generally collected in nets and pressed between heavy stone wheels or millstones to produce the oil from the flesh of the fruit. Some mills use stainless steel units and hydraulic presses in place of the screw presses. This has affected both the quality of the oil and the yield. The older presses extracted around 40% of the oil at the first pressing (or cold pressing). To this, hot water was added and it was pressed again for the second pressing (or hot pressing). The modern machinery used today extracts over 90% of oil from the first pressing, the remaining pulp being sent on for further processing, thus eliminating the second pressing.

Once harvested, the olives are separated from the leaves and washed thoroughly. They are then crushed between two millstones and formed into a paste. The process continues for 30 minutes, during which time the oil is released from the olives. The paste is then spread over round woven mats, which are piled up and put on to a hydraulic press. The oil trickles through the mats to be collected at the base of the press. The oil produced is reddish brown in colour, consisting of olive oil and olive vegetable water. The two are then separated in a centrifuge and the oil is stored immediately underground in tanks. The traditional method of decanting the mixture into troughs and skimming the oil from the surface is still used in some areas, and this oil can be recognized by the word Affiorato on the label. Any oil produced that does not reach the standard required is sent to the refinery for further processing and cleaning.

Some of the smaller, single-estate farms extract the first-run oil before the paste is pressed. This oil is of the best quality and highly priced, being bottled and sealed by hand and numbered; it can be recognized by the words Yema flor on the label, or 'yolk flower'.

Another method commonly used to produce very high-quality oil is one whereby the olive paste is passed over thousands of moving stainless steel blades; the oil sticks to the blades and is funnelled off.

The Grading of Olive Oil

Only around 10% of the world's olive oil production is virgin oil; the rest is refined to remove impurities that would affect the final quality of the oil. Oils are graded by their level of acidity, and this is done both by tasting and by chemical means. Generally speaking, oils with the lower acidity levels are the finer oils. Extra-virgin olive oil is top quality and is unprocessed oil with an acidity level of no more than 1% and a good flavour, aroma and colour. Fine virgin has an acidity level no higher than 1.5%. Virgin oil has an acidity level no higher than 2% and a good colour, aroma and flavour. Olive oil is a blend of virgin and refined oils and has an acidity level no higher than 1.5%. As refined oil has no flavour or colour, the virgin oil gives it these attributes and is added in varying quantities, altering its flavour. Olive pomace oil is refined oil extracted from the pomace or paste, which is left on the hydraulic presses. The oil will have an acidity level no greater than 1.5% and is given its flavour by the addition of extra-virgin olive oil.

*G*enerally speaking, Spanish oils are rich and nutty, or fruity. Lerida and Borjas Blancas are characteristically nutty and they may be peppery but sweet. Siurana oils are not as peppery, whereas the Baena oils are very fruity and smooth. The Jaen and Sierra de Segura oils are fruity with a slight bitterness.

Italian oils can vary, being fruity, nutty, peppery or sweet. The Ligurian oils are lemony and sweet, while the Tuscan oils are rich and fruity with pepper and chocolate overtones, with a strong green colouring. The oils from the central region of Italy (Umbria, Molise and Abruzzi) and the island of Sardinia are full in flavour and slightly sweet and peppery. The oils of the south are traditionally peppery and thick.

Greek oils are grassy, smelling of hay. They are plainer in flavour and can be slightly peppery. French oils are sweet and milder, with fruit flavours and aromas, while the Californian oils are milder and sweeter.

Although olive oils are valued for their aroma and flavour, there are obviously many variations of oil from around the world, each having its particular characteristic, rather like a wine. Some say a peppery oil is superior, but this is clearly a case of personal taste. The characteristics of an oil will depend upon its country or region of origin, though there is still variation within these regions. The only way to discover your preferred oil is by tasting and finding one which suits your particular likes and dislikes.

Cooking with Olive Oil

In Mediterranean countries, olive oil is vital to the native cuisine and is used almost as much as a seasoning as a cooking medium. Its uses are varied: it may be drizzled into soups as a finishing touch, as a base for a sauce or dip, or as a lubricant for frying, roasting or grilling. It is worthwhile buying the best oil you can, in order to improve the flavour of your cooking.

Olive oil can be used for shallow and deep-frying and may be heated on more than one occasion without losing its fine qualities. The smoking point is the same as for corn oil, but it can actually be heated repeatedly, unlike other oils, as it does not break down in the same way.

California. It is excellent mixed with an acidic fruit, such as lemon or lime, then brushed over grilled (broiled) meats or drizzled over barbecued meat and fish, as the heat of the food brings out the flavour of the oil.

One of the latest ideas is to infuse olive oil with a herb or flavouring, such as garlic or sun-dried tomato. This can be added to your cooking for extra flavour or to enhance the flavour when the oil is used as a table condiment. Of course, olive oil is also used as a medium in which to store peppers, chilli, olives and roasted vegetables.

If you are using the oil as a flavouring on the table, then buy the best oil you can afford. Drizzle the oil over salads, pasta, soups and vegetables or use as a dressing base mixed with vinegar and lemon. Olive oil can be used to make sauces and, of course, mayonnaise, for which you may need to use a lighter oil than extra-virgin for a milder flavour. Olive oil is also used straight from the bottle as a sauce on its own in Mediterranean countries and in

Olive oil is also added to breads and cakes to give them a delicious flavour, and is widely used in pasta dishes as a sauce base or as an important ingredient. Throughout the Mediterranean region, Greece, Turkey, Spain, North Africa, America and now the southern hemisphere, olive oil is used in a wide variety of ways to enhance an enormous number of dishes. These are reflected in the following chapters of the book, where a wide variety of recipes for all occasions, and from various countries, are given for your enjoyment and full appreciation of olive oil.

The Keeping Properties of Olive Oil

Olive oil needs to be stored in a dark, preferably cool place to prevent it from going rancid quickly. If you are unable to do this, the oil should be used fairly quickly. Although it needs to be in a cool place, the oil should not be stored in the refrigerator, as it will turn cloudy and begin to solidify. (This state will be reversed once the oil is placed back in warmer conditions). If kept correctly, the oil will last for a year after harvest, so 'best before' dates should be checked before purchasing your oil. You will quickly be able to tell if your oil is turning rancid, as it will have an unpleasant smell, and should be discarded.

The Health Benefits of Olive Oil

It is now widely publicized that the Mediterranean-style diet, based largely on the use of olive oil, is a healthy eating style that should be adopted by us all. Made up of about 70% monounsaturated fatty acids, olive oil also contains vitamin E, an antioxidant important for the prevention of cancers. It does not contain the dreaded cholesterol, which most of us need to reduce in our diets, and is a great source of energy. In fact, olive oil is believed to reduce the amount of cholesterol in the blood and thereby the risk of heart disease, by reducing the 'unhelpful' blood cholesterol and leaving the 'helpful' blood cholesterol levels stable.

The oil is also helpful to the digestive system, particularly the gall bladder, where it is believed to protect against the formation of gall stones. It aids the assimilation of minerals and vitamins, which are essential to our health and well-being in general, and may be helpful to those suffering from non-insulin dependent diabetes. The oil may also be used as a mild laxative.

Olives contain vitamins A and E, phosphorus, potassium, magnesium and manganese, as well as the antioxidants oleic and linoleic acid. Black olives are more readily digested and have a higher vitamin and antioxidant content than green olives. Research has shown that those of us who follow a diet rich in olives or olive oil and also low in animal fat have a reduced risk of cardiovascular disease. The oleic acid content in olive oil is said to regulate the levels of good high density lipoprotein (HDL) and bad low density lipoprotein (LDL) cholesterol in the blood, so reducing the risk of cardiovascular disease. The olive leaves can be used as a remedy for high blood pressure and bladder stones, diabetes and angina, and when used on the skin the oil can aid recovery from psoriasis, eczema and dry skin.

Different Oils
Available on the Market

A l'olivier

Created by M Popelin, a French chemist, the company was bought and moved to Provence in France. They buy extra-virgin olive oils and blend them to produce a good consistent flavour. The oils have a good lemony flavour and are slightly peppery, ideal for all-round cooking.

Antinori

The history of these producers reaches back over 600 years, and the oils are produced in the Chianti region of Italy. The quality of the oil is good and has improved over recent years. They use Frantoio, Leccino and Moraiolo olives, and they have three farms in the region producing a blended oil, the *Laudemio Tenuta Marchese Antinori*. Crushed in the traditional manner at a stone mill, the olive oil is made only from the olives grown on the farm, and they are processed by the cold centrifugal method. The oil has a fragrant aroma of newly mown grass, and the flavour is nutty but with a sweet aftertaste. The Peppoli farm produces an extra-virgin oil with a herbaceous aroma and nutty, peppery flavour.

Ardoino and Isnardl

Two long-established businesses that joined forces to produce fine extra-virgin oils. The company previously sold to America and now produces fine oils for discerning clients. The Taggiasca olives used to make the oil are grown in the high valley of Oneglia, and the harvest is from November to May. Poles are used to knock the olives into nets, from where they are taken to be milled. The oil is not filtered and has a lemony aroma with a strong presence of almonds. Ardoino Biancardo is one of the rarest oils in the world and produced when the Taggiasca olives are left to mature until May. Ardoino Fructus is a blend of oils made from other Mediterranean oils and the Taggiasca olive.

Athena

This Greek oil is produced from olives farmed as co-operatives in the Kalamata and Messinia regions, without the use of pesticides. They are harvested before fully ripe and processed by both traditional and centrifugal methods. The resulting oil has a nutty flavour, which is on the bitter side.

Badia a Coltibuono

The estate that produces this oil is a family-run business, situated in the heart of the Chianti region. With a monastery at the centre of the estate, olive oil production is carried out alongside a cookery school run by Lorenza de Medici, the wife of the owner Pietro. The oils produced are first-class, extra-virgin oils.

The olives used are Frantoio, Leccino and Pendolino. These are harvested early and pressed using traditional methods, before being filtered through cotton wool. The Badia Coltibuono extra-virgin oil has a fruity aroma and flavour with a hint of nuts, while the Badia Albereto extra-virgin oil has a sharper aroma and tastes slightly bitter and peppery.

Bartolini

This estate has produced an award-winning extra-virgin oil. It primarily uses the Moraiolo olive with the Frantoio and Leccino as back-up olives. They are hand-picked and processed using the centrifugal method. The extra-virgin olive oil has a nutty and spicy aroma, the flavour being a mixture of nuts, coffee and pepper. Suitable for all culinary uses, it is a smooth, versatile oil.

Borelli

This is a relatively new company, but a major producer not only in Italy, but in Canada, France and the USA. It is associated with Carbonell in Spain. They produce a range of oils including the Borelli extra-virgin oil, Ligurian and Tuscan speciality oils. The Ligurian extra-virgin oil uses only Taggiasca olives, and the Taggiasca extra-virgin oil has a nutty aroma and tastes slightly sweet with a hint of apples, although slightly peppery. The Tuscan extra-virgin oil is pressed from a blend of olives: the Frantoio, Leccino and Moraiolo. The fruits are harvested between December and January and are pressed using traditional methods.

The Borelli extra-virgin oil has a sweet and citrus aroma, and is best used very fresh.

Borges

A Spanish producer, and one of the largest, collecting olives from all around the valleys of Catalonia. They are used to produce an extra-virgin olive oil with an intense, fruity and eggy aroma. It is slightly sweet in flavour, with a peppery, slightly bitter aftertaste. It is an oil with definite qualities, which should be used with strongly flavoured foods.

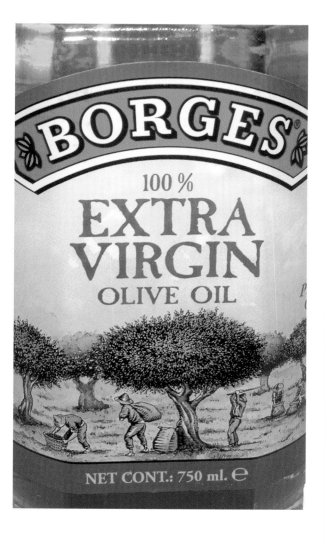

Bottarelli

Produced from olives grown in the hills around Lake Garda, this extra-virgin olive oil is made from Easalivia and Leccino olives, producing a fruity oil with the flavour and aroma of apples and lemons. It is not very peppery and is suitable for most culinary uses.

Carapelli

This is the leading olive oil brand in Italy, producing 46 million litres (about 10 million gallons) a year. Carapelli Oro Verde extra-virgin olive oil has a grassy aroma and flavour, which is quite peppery and has a tangy aftertaste. Ideal for salad dressings or for use in marinades for meat and poultry.

Colonna

The estate is situated just south of Rome, and grows several different varieties of olive, including Coratina, Leccino, Ascolano, Nocellara and Peranzana. All varieties are harvested, milled and pressed separately to produce consistently good, blended oils. Harvesting takes place between October and December, and is mainly carried out by machine just before the olives are ripe, after which they are immediately processed. Once milled, the paste is passed over stainless steel blades to give a pure oil. The Colonna extra-virgin oil has a fresh aroma of olives, the taste being grassy with a peppery aftertaste. The estate also produces a fine lemon-flavoured oil called Granverde; Mandarino, a mandarin-flavoured oil; and Arancio an orange-flavoured oil.

Carbonell

Excellent olive oils are produced here year after year and these are sold all over the world. Blending oils are produced from the Arbequina, Hojiblanca, Picaul and Picudo olives, which are hand-picked and processed using the centrifugal method. The extra-virgin oil has a sweet and fruity aroma, with a less intense flavour. It is a great oil to use for most culinary purposes.

Cypressa

This is the name for the extra-virgin olive oil produced from Kalamata olives grown in the Lakonia area of Greece. The olives are hand-picked between October and January and processed using the cold centrifugal system. The resultant oil has aromas of leaves and nuts and a flavour that is peppery with a nutty aftertaste. The company also imports an extra-virgin oil called Eleanthos, with grassy aromas and nutty flavours.

Fillipo Berio

Now one of Italy's leading oil producers, this name is familiar to most of us. The company used to be a smaller concern, buying olives from local farmers and selling them on to Italian immigrants in the USA and northern Europe. The company now buys olive oil from all over Italy and from other countries and blends a range of oils that is marketed around the world. The extra-virgin oil has a fruity aroma and flavour, which is slightly nutty with a peppery aftertaste. Some years, they produce a quickly pressed 'nuovo' extra-virgin oil, which is very bitter and punchy.

The Frantoio Olive Oil Company

This company produces olive oils in both Italy and California. Mission, Manzanillo and Ascolana olives are brought in from northern California and crushed and pressed in the company's restaurant. The Frantoio extra-virgin olive oil is a blend of Manzanillo autumn oil and Mission winter oil. They also press oils from 100% Ascolano, Sevillano, Picholine or Barouni olives for other estates. The Italian oil has a delicious flavour, combining nuts, chocolate and citrus, with a peppery and nutty aftertaste.

Recipes from Around the Globe

Minestrone Soup with Pesto

Serves 4

150 g/5 oz/1 cup dried flageolet beans, soaked overnight

2 large potatoes, chopped

3 large carrots, diced

2 leeks, chopped

2 celery sticks, chopped

2 large tomatoes, chopped

1 green (bell) pepper, chopped

3 courgettes (zucchini), chopped

450 g/1 lb/4½ cups green cabbage, shredded

3 tablespoons olive oil

225 g/8 oz macaroni

freshly ground black pepper

60 g/2 oz/½ cup freshly grated Parmesan cheese

For the pesto

2 garlic cloves

2 tablespoons pine nuts

30 fresh basil leaves

freshly ground black pepper

30 g/1 oz/¼ cup freshly grated Parmesan cheese

3 tablespoons olive oil

Heat 1 litre/1¾ pints/4¼ cups water in a large saucepan and add all the prepared vegetables, including the beans. Add the olive oil and cook over a gentle heat for 1¼ hours, or until the beans have cooked.

Meanwhile, make the pesto sauce. Place all the sauce ingredients in a food processor or blender and blend until well mixed and a paste is formed.

Add the pasta to the soup and cook for 8 minutes. Stir the pesto sauce into the soup, then season to taste and sprinkle with Parmesan cheese. Serve immediately.

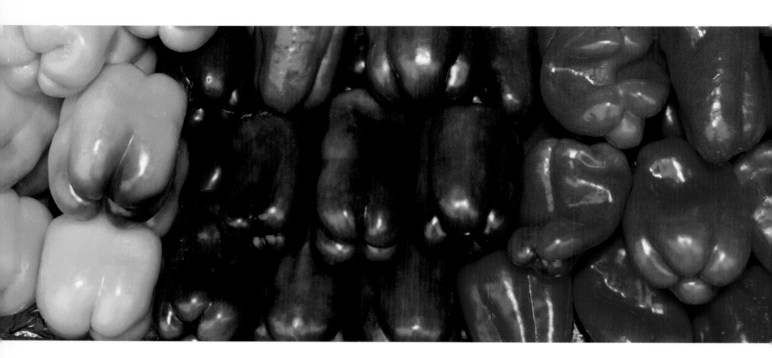

Peppers with Anchovy Sauce

Serves 4

3 yellow (bell) peppers
3 green (bell) peppers
5 garlic cloves
90 g/3 oz anchovy fillets
6 tablespoons olive oil
mixed freshly chopped herbs
freshly ground black pepper

Roast the peppers over a gas flame or place under a grill (broiler), skin-side uppermost until the skins char and blister. Peel the skins from the peppers and discard. Seed the peppers and cut the peppers into thin strips.

Place all the remaining ingredients in a food processor or blender and blend until smooth.

Arrange the peppers in a serving dish and pour the anchovy sauce over the top. Garnish with herbs and serve.

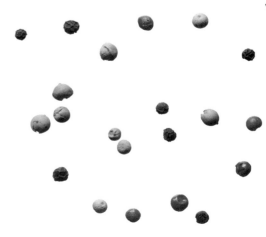

Mixed Fish Soup

Serves 4

1 kg/2¼ lb uncooked prawns (shrimps)
225 g/8 oz white fish fillets
2 litres/3½ pints/2¼ quarts fresh fish stock
450 g/1 lb/3 cups plum tomatoes, chopped
4 tablespoons olive oil
4 anchovy fillets, chopped
3 garlic cloves, chopped
2 tablespoons freshly chopped dill or chervil
8 thick slices French bread
freshly ground black pepper

Remove the shells and heads from the prawns, and clean thoroughly. Skin the white fish and cut the fish into cubes. Place the stock in a large saucepan and heat gently.

Rub the tomatoes through a sieve (strainer) and add to the stock.

Heat the oil in a separate, large pan and add the anchovies, garlic and herbs. As soon as the garlic begins to brown slightly, add the stock, then reduce the heat and simmer for 25 minutes.

Add the prawns and fish to the stock and cook for 5 minutes until the prawns turn pink.

Meanwhile, toast the bread slices under the grill (broiler) and place two pieces in the base of each serving dish.

Season the soup to taste and ladle over the toasted bread. Serve immediately.

Penne with Anchovies and Tomatoes

Serves 4

275 g/10 oz plum tomatoes
3½ tablespoons olive oil
1 tablespoon freshly chopped marjoram
4 anchovy fillets
3 garlic cloves, crushed
125 ml/4 fl oz/½ cup single (light) cream
freshly ground black pepper
225 g/8 oz penne
marjoram to garnish

Cut the tomatoes in half and sprinkle with 1/2 tablespoon of the olive oil and half of the marjoram. Cook under a medium grill (broiler) for 2–3 minutes, or until soft. Skin the tomatoes and chop the flesh.

Chop the anchovies and sauté in the remaining olive oil with the garlic until the anchovies disintegrate.

Add the cream to the pan and stir until it begins to bubble, then add the tomatoes and season to taste with pepper.

Meanwhile, cook the pasta in boiling salted water for 8–10 minutes, or until al dente. Drain well and stir into the sauce with the remaining marjoram. Serve immediately.

Pasta with Broccoli and Anchovy Crust

Serves 4

For the anchovy crust

2 tablespoons olive oil

4 anchovy fillets, chopped

1 garlic clove, crushed

2 thick slices white bread

For the pasta

450 g/1 lb broccoli, cut into small florets

1 red (bell) pepper, seeded and chopped

4 tablespoons olive oil

3 garlic cloves, crushed

350 g/12 oz pasta twists

freshly ground black pepper

freshly grated Parmesan cheese to serve

To make the anchovy crust, heat the oil in a frying pan (skillet) and sauté the anchovies and garlic until the anchovies disintegrate. Break the bread into pieces and add to the pan, turning until the bread is crisp. Remove from the heat and reserve.

Meanwhile, cook the broccoli and red pepper in boiling water until tender, then drain. Return to the pan with the oil and garlic and cook for 1–2 minutes.

Meanwhile, cook the pasta in boiling salted water for 8–10 minutes, or until al dente. Drain and add to the pan with the broccoli and garlic, then cook for 1–2 minutes, stirring. Season to taste.

Return the anchovy crust to the heat and warm through. Spoon the pasta into individual serving dishes and sprinkle the anchovy crust over the top. Serve with Parmesan cheese.

Aubergine Rolls

Serves 4

2 small aubergines (eggplants)

6 tablespoons olive oil

3 tablespoons red wine vinegar

1 tablespoon balsamic vinegar

2 anchovy fillets

3 garlic cloves, crushed

2 tablespoons freshly chopped oregano

1 red onion, finely chopped

2 tablespoons capers

freshly ground black pepper

oregano to garnish

Trim the ends from the aubergines and stand the aubergines on their ends. Using a very sharp knife, cut the thinnest possible slices from the aubergines and place on a plate. Sprinkle a little salt over the aubergines and leave to stand for 20 minutes. Rinse under cold water and pat dry with paper (towels).

Heat 3 tablespoons of the oil in a large frying pan (skillet) and cook half of the aubergines in the oil, turning once until they begin to brown. Remove from the pan and roll up. Place in a serving dish.

Add another 2 tablespoons of the oil and cook the remaining aubergines, then roll up and place in the serving dish.

Mix the remaining oil, the vinegars and the anchovies and add to the pan. Cook until the anchovies dissolve. Stir in the garlic, herbs, onion and capers and cook for 4–5 minutes. Season with black pepper and pour over the aubergine rolls. Leave to cool completely, then garnish with oregano and serve.

Grilled Goat's Cheese

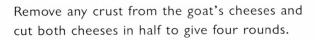

Serves 4

2 round goat's cheeses
1 tablespoon red wine vinegar
3 tablespoons olive oil
freshly ground black pepper
1 tablespoon freshly chopped parsley
1 garlic clove, thinly sliced
mixed salad leaves for serving

Remove any crust from the goat's cheeses and cut both cheeses in half to give four rounds.

Transfer the cheese to a shallow ovenproof dish. Mix the vinegar, oil, black pepper, parsley and garlic and pour over the cheese.

Cook under a medium grill (broiler) until the cheese begins to brown and melt slightly.

Arrange the salad leaves on four serving plates and place a round of cheese on top. Pour over a little of the oil mixture and serve immediately.

Fried Radicchio and Chicory

Serves 4

2 heads radicchio
2 heads chicory
30 g/1 oz/2 tablespoons butter
3 tablespoons olive oil
1 garlic clove, crushed
1 tablespoon pine nuts
1 tablespoon freshly chopped coriander (cilantro)
freshly ground black pepper

Wash the radicchio and chicory and cut each into quarters. Heat the butter and oil in a large frying pan (skillet) and add the garlic and pine nuts. Cook for 1 minute, stirring.

Add the radicchio and chicory and cook for 4–5 minutes, turning to coat in the oil.

Stir in the coriander and season well. Serve immediately.

Vine Leaf Bake

Serves 4

12 vine leaves

3 tablespoons olive oil

2 garlic cloves, crushed

8 field mushrooms, peeled and chopped

2 tablespoons freshly chopped parsley

1 red (bell) pepper, peeled and thinly sliced

ground black pepper

Wash the vine leaves and lay four in the base of an ovenproof dish. Mix the oil and garlic and spoon a third of the mixture over the vine leaves.

Mix the mushrooms, parsley and red pepper and season well. Spoon half of the mixture on to the vine leaves and lay another four leaves on top to cover.

Sprinkle with a third of the oil and top with the remaining mushroom mixture. Lay the remaining vine leaves on top of the mixture to cover completely and pour on the remaining oil and garlic.

Heat the oven to 180°C/350°F/Gas 4. Cover the dish with baking foil and cook in the oven for 25 minutes. Remove the foil and cook for another 5 minutes. Serve immediately.

Polenta with Peppers

Serves 4

½ teaspoon salt

125 g/4 oz/1 cup polenta

1 tablespoon freshly chopped basil

1 tablespoon freshly chopped parsley

30 g/1 oz/2 tablespoons butter

60 g/2 oz/ ½ cup freshly grated Parmesan cheese

2 green (bell) peppers, peeled and seeded

1 red (bell) pepper, peeled and seeded

3 tablespoons olive oil

2 garlic cloves, crushed

90 g/3 oz/1½ cups rocket (arugula)

3 tablespoons white wine

2 teaspoons garlic vinegar

basil leaves to garnish

Bring 600ml/1pint/2½ cups water to the boil and add the salt. Whisk the polenta into the water and cook for 20 minutes over a gentle heat.

Stir in the basil, parsley, butter and Parmesan cheese, and pour into an oiled square tin. Set aside to cool.

Meanwhile, cut the peppers into strips. Cut the polenta into triangles and brush with oil. Cook under a medium grill (broiler) for 5 minutes on each side.

Heat the remaining oil in a frying pan (skillet) and cook the garlic and peppers for 2–3 minutes, stirring. Add the rocket, wine and vinegar and mix well.

Remove the pan from the heat and spoon the mixture on to a serving plate. Top with polenta triangles and basil and serve immediately.

Marinated Peppers

Makes 2 jars

1 green (bell) pepper
1 red (bell) pepper
1 yellow (bell) pepper
3 shallots, finely chopped
2 rosemary sprigs
2 marjoram sprigs
4 garlic cloves, chopped
1 tablespoon mixed peppercorns
6 tablespoons lemon or lime juice
250 ml/8 fl oz/1 cup olive oil
6 tablespoons white wine or vermouth

Cut the peppers into very thin strips of even length and pack into two preserving jars with lids. Add the shallots, herbs, garlic and peppercorns, dividing evenly between the two jars.

Mix the lemon or lime juice with the oil and wine or vermouth and pour into the jars.

Seal with tightly fitting lids and store for at least 24 hours before using. They will keep for up to 3 weeks.

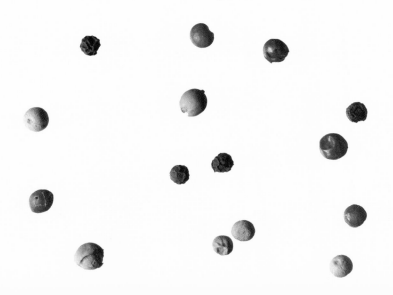

Gazpacho

Serves 6

1 cucumber
450 g/1 lb tomatoes, peeled
1 green (bell) pepper, seeded
1 red onion
2 garlic cloves, crushed
5 tablespoons olive oil
4 tablespoons red wine vinegar
400 ml/14 fl oz/1¾ cups passata
2 tablespoons tomato purée (paste)
basil leaves to garnish

Roughly chop the cucumber, tomatoes, pepper and onion, reserving a few pieces for garnish. Place the roughly chopped vegetables in a mixing bowl and add the garlic.

Stir in the remaining ingredients and transfer to a food processor or blender. Blend until smooth. You may have to do this in batches.

Transfer the blended soup into a serving bowl, then cover and chill well.

Ladle into individual serving bowls and garnish with the reserved vegetables and basil leaves. If liked, add two ice cubes to each serving for a really cool soup.

Garlic Soup

Serves 4

1.15 litres/2 pints/5 cups chicken stock

1 medium-sized potato, peeled and diced

2 onions, diced

5 tomatoes, skinned and chopped

1 large carrot, chopped

2 celery sticks, chopped

450 g/1 lb green beans, chopped

freshly ground black pepper

5 garlic cloves

3 tablespoons olive oil

1 tablespoon freshly chopped basil

Place the stock in a large saucepan and bring to the boil. Add the vegetables and simmer for 15–20 minutes. Season well.

Crush the garlic and add to the soup with the oil and basil. Cook for another 10 minutes, or until the vegetables are quite tender. Serve, garnished with basil.

Tapenade

Serves 4

225 g/8 oz/2 cups pitted black olives

1 tablespoon capers

1 anchovy fillet

4 tablespoons olive oil

2 teaspoons lemon juice

½ teaspoon prepared mustard

2 garlic cloves, crushed

2 teaspoons freshly chopped parsley

freshly ground black pepper

Wash the olives and place in a food processor
with the remaining ingredients. Blend well
until smooth and transfer to a serving dish.

Chill until required and serve with thin toast.

Bean Dip

Serves 4

225 g/8 oz/2 cups shelled broad (fava) beans

3 garlic cloves, crushed

1 tablespoon freshly grated Parmesan cheese

1 tablespoon freshly chopped parsley

4 tablespoons olive oil

Cook the beans in boiling water until tender. Drain well.

Transfer to a food processor with the remaining ingredients and blend until smooth.

Transfer to a serving dish and drizzle a little more olive oil over the top. Serve with crudités or thin toast.

Middle Eastern Roast Chicken

Serves 4

1.5 kg/3¼ lb oven-ready roasting chicken

For the marinade

200 ml/7 fl oz/¾ cup olive oil

4 tablespoons lemon juice

1 teaspoon salt

freshly ground black pepper

½ teaspoon turmeric

½ teaspoon ground cumin

½ teaspoon ground coriander

pinch of ground ginger

1 tablespoon freshly chopped mint

Wash the chicken inside and out and pat dry with paper towels. Place in a roasting pan.

Mix the marinade ingredients together and rub all over the chicken. Leave the chicken to marinate for at least 3 hours, but no longer than 24 hours, basting occasionally.

Heat the oven to 190°C/375°F/Gas 5. Place the chicken on a rack over a roasting pan and cook in the oven for 1 hour, occasionally basting with any reserved marinade.

Increase the oven temperature to 220°C/425°F/Gas 7 and cook for another 10 minutes to brown and crispen slightly.

Remove the chicken from the oven and leave to stand for 15 minutes before carving.

Chicken Tagine with Honey and Dates

Serves 4

4 tablespoons olive oil

2 medium-sized onions, chopped

2 garlic cloves, crushed

½ teaspoon ground coriander

½ teaspoon ground cumin

large pinch of ground ginger

½ teaspoon turmeric

1 teaspoon cumin seeds

2 bay leaves

675 g/1½ lb lean chicken meat, cubed

16 fresh dates, seeded and quartered

125 g/4 oz/1 cup blanched whole almonds

2 tablespoons clear honey

In a heavy-based saucepan, heat the oil and fry the onion, garlic, spices and cumin seeds for 15 minutes over a low heat, stirring occasionally.

Add 600 ml/1 pint/2½ cups boiling water and the bay leaves, then simmer, uncovered, for 30 minutes, or until the liquid has reduced by a third.

Add the chicken and simmer for another 20 minutes, stirring occasionally.

Stir in the dates, almonds and honey, then simmer for another 10 minutes and serve with freshly steamed couscous or rice.

Sesame Chicken

Serves 4

For the marinade

8 tablespoons olive oil

4 tablespoons tahini

½ teaspoon paprika pepper

3 garlic cloves, crushed

1 teaspoon turmeric

1 teaspoon ground cumin

For the chicken

4 chicken breast fillets, skinned and cut into thin strips

60 g/2 oz /½ cup sesame seeds

Mix the marinade ingredients together to a smooth paste. Place the chicken in a glass dish and pour the marinade over, turning the chicken to coat in the marinade. Leave to marinate for at least 3 hours, but no longer than 24 hours.

Preheat the oven to 160°C/325°F/Gas 3. Spread the sesame seeds on a baking sheet and cook in the oven for about 10 minutes, or until golden brown.

Remove the chicken from the marinade and roll each strip in the sesame seeds to coat completely.

Transfer the chicken to a shallow baking dish and pour any remaining marinade over the top. Sprinkle with the remaining sesame seeds and cook in the oven for 20 minutes, or until the chicken is cooked through. Serve hot with a salad of your choice.

Sherried Garlic Chicken

Serves 4

8 small chicken portions or
1.5k g/3¼ lb chicken cut into portions
1 teaspoon paprika pepper
salt and freshly ground black pepper
6 tablespoons olive oil
8 garlic cloves, chopped
1 onion, halved and sliced
1 tablespoon brandy
125 ml/4 fl oz/½ cup dry sherry
1 bay leaf
1 tablespoon freshly chopped marjoram

Rub the chicken portions with paprika, salt and pepper.

Heat the oil in a large flameproof casserole and fry the garlic until lightly browned. Remove the garlic from the casserole and add the onion and chicken portions. Cook for 5 minutes, turning until the chicken is browned on all sides.

Return the garlic to the pan and pour in the brandy and sherry. Stir in the bay leaves and marjoram and bring to the boil.

Reduce the heat, then cover and simmer for 45 minutes, or until the chicken is tender. Serve with freshly boiled rice.

Chicken with Almonds

Serves 4

4 chicken portions
salt and freshly ground black pepper
5 tablespoons olive oil
5 garlic cloves, crushed
25 blanched whole almonds
pinch of ground cinnamon
pinch of ground cumin
1 tablespoon freshly chopped parsley
1 teaspoon peppercorns
a few saffron strands or turmeric
1 teaspoon salt
1 red onion, chopped
3 tablespoons water
300 ml/½ pint/1¼ cups dry white wine
1 bay leaf

Season the chicken with salt and pepper. Heat the oil in a pan and cook the garlic and almonds for a few minutes, stirring until golden. Transfer to a food processor or blender, and add the spices, parsley, peppercorns, saffron or turmeric, and salt, then blend to a paste with a little water if necessary.

Reheat the oil in the pan and cook the chicken and onion until lightly browned on all sides. Add the almond paste and remaining water, wine and bay leaf, then bring to the boil. Reduce the heat, cover and simmer for 45 minutes, or until the chicken is cooked through. Serve hot with rice.

Chicken with Peppers

Serves 4

1.5 kg/3¼ lb chicken, cut into portions
salt and freshly ground black pepper
2 green (bell) peppers
3 red (bell) peppers
6 tablespoons olive oil
4 garlic cloves, chopped
225 g/8 oz Spanish sausage, sliced
2 onions, chopped
5 tomatoes, skinned
2 tablespoons freshly chopped parsley

Rub the chicken portions all over with salt and pepper.

Put the peppers under a grill (broiler), skin-side uppermost, and grill (broil) until the skins char and blister. Remove from the grill and peel the skins from the peppers. Seed the peppers and cut the flesh into strips.

Heat the oil in a flameproof casserole and fry the chicken, turning until golden brown all over. Add the garlic, sausage and onions and cook until the onions begin to soften.

Stir in the tomatoes and peppers and cook for 30 minutes over a low heat until the chicken is tender and the sauce has thickened. Stir in the parsley and serve.

Rabbit in Red Wine

Serves 4

2 rabbits, divided into portions

250 ml/8 fl oz/1 cup chicken stock

2 tablespoons red wine vinegar

4 tablespoons Marsala

6 tablespoons olive oil

salt and freshly ground black pepper

2 tablespoons freshly chopped marjoram

1 bay leaf

2 onions, sliced

3 garlic cloves, crushed

400 g/14 oz can plum tomatoes

250 ml/8 fl oz/1 cup dry red wine

500 g/16 oz potatoes

Soak the rabbit portions in the stock and vinegar overnight. Drain and pat dry with paper towels. Place the rabbit in a shallow bowl and pour the Marsala over. Leave to marinate for 2–3 hours.

Heat the oil in a large frying pan (skillet). Season the rabbit with salt and pepper and fry in the oil for 20 minutes, turning until golden brown all over. Transfer the rabbit to a casserole, with any remaining marinade and the herbs.

Add the onions to the frying pan and cook until soft. Stir in the garlic, tomatoes and wine and heat through to break up the tomatoes. Bring to the boil and pour over the rabbit in the casserole.

Heat the oven to 180°C/350°F/Gas 4. Cover and cook the rabbit casserole for 1 hour, or until the rabbit is tender.

Cut the potatoes into chips and add to the casserole, making sure they are immersed in sauce. Return to the oven and cook for another 30 minutes, until tender. Serve.

Chicken with Olives

Serves 4

1.5 kg/3¼ lb oven-ready chicken with giblets

1 onion, chopped

3 tablespoons olive oil

2 garlic cloves, crushed

pinch of ground ginger

½ teaspoon turmeric

½ teaspoon ground cumin

150 ml/¼ pint/⅔ cup chicken stock

3 tomatoes, seeded and chopped

the chicken liver

2 preserved lemons, chopped

2 tablespoons black pitted olives, quartered

2 tablespoons freshly chopped coriander (cilantro)

Cut the chicken into portions and reserve. Fry the onions in the oil in a heavy saucepan until softened. Add the garlic, ginger, turmeric and cumin. Cook for another 1 minute and pour in the stock.

Place the chicken pieces, tomatoes and liver into the pan and cook gently, turning the chicken pieces until the chicken is almost off the bone and really tender.

Remove the chicken from the pan and remove the liver. Mash the liver and return it to the pan. Bring the sauce to the boil to reduce and thicken.

Add the preserved lemons, olives and coriander and heat through. Serve the chicken with the sauce spooned over the top.

Threaded Chicken

Serves 4
4 boneless chicken breasts, skinned
5 tablespoons olive oil
3 garlic cloves, crushed
juice of 1 lime
freshly ground black pepper
2 limes, each cut into eight

Cut the chicken into 2.5 cm/1 inch cubes.
Mix the oil, garlic, lime and pepper, then pour
over the chicken cubes and leave to marinate
for 2 hours.

Thread the chicken cubes and lime quarters
on to skewers and cook under a medium grill
(broiler) for 10–12 minutes, turning and
brushing with the marinade, until the chicken
is cooked through.

Serve immediately, with green salad leaves.

Chicken with Walnuts

Serves 4
1 kg/2¼ lb chicken, cut into small pieces
salt and freshly ground black pepper
2 tablespoons flour
6 tablespoons olive oil
1 red onion, finely chopped
16 shelled walnuts
2 garlic cloves
125 ml/4 fl oz/½ cup milk
125 ml/4 fl oz/½ cup white wine or vermouth
475 ml/16 fl oz/2 cups chicken stock
1 tablespoon freshly chopped parsley

Rub the chicken pieces with salt and pepper and coat them with flour. Heat the oil in a large frying pan (skillet) and cook the chicken, turning until browned all over.

Add the onion and cook until softened.

Meanwhile, pound the walnuts to a paste with the garlic cloves and add the milk to make a creamy consistency.

Stir the walnut cream into the pan with the wine or vermouth, add the stock and cook over a low heat for 30 minutes, or until the chicken is cooked through and the sauce has thickened. Sprinkle the parsley over the chicken and serve immediately.

Saffron Turkey

Serves 4

5 garlic cloves
20 whole almonds, blanched
5 tablespoons olive oil
3 tablespoons coriander (cilantro) leaves
675 g/1½ lb turkey fillets, cut into cubes
salt and freshly ground black pepper
3 tablespoons flour
1 red onion, chopped
1 celery stick, chopped
250 ml/8 fl oz/1 cup sherry
1 bay leaf
350 ml/12 fl oz/1½ cups chicken stock
1 teaspoon saffron threads
1 teaspoon turmeric
2 (hard-cooked) boiled eggs

Fry the garlic and almonds in the oil, stirring until browned. Add the coriander leaves and cook for a few seconds. Remove the garlic, almonds and coriander from the pan and then pound in a pestle and mortar.

Season the turkey and toss it in the flour to coat. Cook in the oil, turning until browned all over. Remove the turkey from the pan and add the onion and celery. Cook until the onion has softened.

Return the turkey to the pan and add the sherry. Cook for 1–2 minutes before adding the bay leaf, chicken stock, saffron and turmeric.

Add the yolks of the eggs to the paste in the mortar and thin the paste with a little of the stock. Stir into the pan and simmer gently for 30 minutes, or until the turkey is cooked through.

Chop the egg whites and sprinkle over the top of the dish just before serving.

Quail in Chocolate Sauce

Serves 4

4 quails, halved
salt and freshly ground black pepper
flour for coating
5 tablespoons olive oil
16 baby onions, peeled
2 celery sticks, cut into matchsticks
1 carrot, cut into matchsticks
1 garlic clove, crushed
600 ml/1 pint/2½ cups chicken stock
2 tablespoons white wine vinegar
8 slices stale French bread
60 g/2 oz/2 squares bitter (semi-sweet) chocolate, grated
celery leaves to garnish

Season the quail and roll them in flour to coat. Heat the oil in a large flameproof casserole and add the quail and onions. Cook, turning until lightly browned.

Add the celery and carrot sticks and the garlic. Cook for 2 minutes. Stir in the stock and vinegar, cover and cook for 45 minutes, or until the quail are tender and cooked through.

Meanwhile, grill the bread slices on both sides and place two on each serving plate. Remove the quail from the casserole and place a portion on each slice of bread.

Remove the carrot and celery from the casserole and arrange on the serving plates.

Stir the chocolate into the sauce and bring to the boil, then pour over the quail and serve immediately, garnished with celery leaves.

Devilled Turkey

Serves 4

5 sun-dried tomatoes in oil, drained and chopped

3 tablespoons tomato chutney

1 teaspoon prepared mustard

1 teaspoon Worcesters sauce

60 g/2 oz/1 cup fresh brown breadcrumbs

4 turkey escalopes (scallops)

2 tablespoons olive oil

1 tablespoon freshly chopped coriander (cilantro)

Heat the oven to 190°C/375°F/Gas 5. Mix the sun-dried tomatoes with the chutney, mustard, Worcester sauce and breadcrumbs. Make slits in each of the turkey escalopes and spread the tomato mixture over one side of each escalope.

Place each coated escalope in a square of foil and drizzle the olive oil over the top.

Fold the foil to make four parcels and place in the oven for 30 minutes, or until the turkey is cooked through.

Open the parcels and cook for another 5 minutes. Serve immediately, sprinkled with coriander.

Duck in Beer

Serves 4

6 tablespoons olive oil

1 medium-sized duck, cut into portions

4 tablespoons gin

5 rashers (slices) streaky bacon, chopped

16 baby onions, peeled

125 g/4 oz button mushrooms

2 tablespoons flour

500 ml/17 fl oz/2¼ cups beer

300 ml/½ pint/1¼ cups chicken stock

1 tablespoon soft brown sugar

1 tablespoon freshly chopped parsley

Heat half of the oil in a large frying pan (skillet) and cook the duck portions until browned on all sides.

Add the gin and ignite, shaking the pan until the flames die back. Transfer the duck to a flameproof casserole.

Add the remaining oil and cook the bacon pieces until they almost begin to crisp. Remove from the pan with a draining spoon and add to the duck in the casserole.

Fry the onions and mushrooms in the same pan and add to the casserole.

Stir the flour into the pan and cook for 2 minutes. Remove from the heat and add the beer and stock.

Stir in the sugar and cook, stirring until the sauce begins to thicken. Season and pour the sauce over the duck. Cover the casserole and cook over a low heat for 40 minutes, or until the duck is cooked through. Serve sprinkled with parsley.

Turkey in Vinegar

Serves 4

4 turkey escalopes (scallops)

salt

150 ml/¼ pint/½ cup olive oil

8 garlic cloves

1 tablespoon paprika pepper

½ teaspoon ground coriander

1 tablespoon freshly chopped oregano

5 tablespoons garlic wine vinegar

300 ml/½ pint/1¼ cups chicken stock

2 tablespoons fresh white breadcrumbs

Season the turkey escalopes with salt. Heat the oil in a large frying pan (skillet) and cook the turkey until golden brown on both sides. Slice four of the garlic cloves and cook in the pan for 2 minutes.

Meanwhile, pound the remaining garlic with the paprika, coriander and oregano to make a paste. Dilute the paste with vinegar and stock. Stir in the breadcrumbs.

Pour over the turkey and cook over a medium heat for 25 minutes, or until the turkey is cooked through and the sauce is quite thick. Serve immediately.

Shish Kebab

Serves 6

750 g/1¾ lb lamb, trimmed and cut into 2.5 cm/1 inch cubes

150 ml/¼ pint/⅔ cup olive oil

1 tablespoon lemon juice

2 onions, grated

2 garlic cloves, crushed

1 bay leaf, crushed

1 tablespoon freshly chopped mint

salt and freshly ground black pepper

Place the cubed meat in a shallow dish. Mix together the oil, lemon juice, onions, garlic, bay leaf and mint and season well. Pour over the meat, turning to coat it well. Cover and leave to marinate for 2 hours.

Remove the meat from the marinade and thread on to six skewers.

Place the skewers under a moderately hot grill (broiler) and cook for 7–10 minutes, turning until cooked through.

Serve garnished with lemon wedges and salad leaves.

Meatballs in Tomato Sauce

Serves 6
For the sauce
2 medium onions, chopped
4 tablespoons olive oil
3 garlic cloves, crushed
750 g/1¾ lb tomatoes, peeled and chopped
1 celery stick, finely chopped
1 teaspoon paprika pepper
½ teaspoon ground cumin
½ teaspoon ground coriander
½ teaspoon ground cinnamon
pinch of ground nutmeg
2 tablespoons freshly chopped mint
300 ml/½ pint/1¼ cups chicken stock
6 eggs
For the meatballs
750 g/1¾ lb minced lamb
1 tablespoon freshly chopped parsley
2 tablespoons freshly chopped coriander (cilantro)
2 teaspoon freshly chopped mint
1 teaspoon paprika pepper
½ teaspoon ground cumin
½ teaspoon ground coriander
½ teaspoon ground ginger

To make the sauce, fry the onions in the oil with the garlic in a large flameproof casserole for 3–4 minutes, stirring. Add the remaining sauce ingredients except the eggs, then simmer for 15 minutes.

Meanwhile, make the meatballs. Mix all the ingredients together in a bowl and bring the mixture together with your hands. Wet your hands and roll the mixture into walnut-sized balls. Add to the sauce and simmer for another 15 minutes.

Break the eggs on to the surface of the sauce and cook for about 10 minutes. Serve.

Lamb with Aubergines

Serves 6

750 g/1¾ lb aubergines (eggplants), cubed
salt and freshly ground black pepper
2 red onions, quartered and sliced
2 garlic cloves, crushed
4 tablespoons olive oil
750 g/1¾ lb lean lamb, cubed
½ teaspoon ground cinnamon
½ teaspoon ground cumin
½ teaspoon ground allspice
pinch of ground ginger
175 g/6 oz/1 cup dried dates, chopped
5 tablespoons white wine vinegar
125 g/4 oz/1 cup whole blanched almonds

Sprinkle the aubergines with salt and leave to stand in a colander over a plate for 20 minutes. Rinse under cold water and pat dry.

Fry the onions and garlic in the oil until softened and add the meat, turning until browned all over.

Stir in the spices and cover with water. Bring to the boil, reduce the heat and simmer for 1 hour.

Add the aubergines and cook for another 30 minutes.

Meanwhile, place the dates and vinegar in a food processor and blend to a smooth cream, adding a little water if required. Pour the sauce over the meat and vegetables, and cook for 2–3 minutes. Serve garnished with the almonds.

Pan-cooked Pork

Serves 4

4 tablespoons olive oil

4 garlic cloves, crushed

450 g/1 lb lean pork, cubed

2 red onions, chopped

1 teaspoon paprika pepper

1 teaspoon turmeric

2 tablespoons freshly chopped marjoram

juice of 1 lemon

salt and freshly ground black pepper

Heat the oil in a flameproof casserole and cook the garlic until browned. Add the pork and cook, turning until evenly browned on all sides.

Add the onions and fry until softened. Stir in the paprika pepper, turmeric, marjoram, lemon juice and seasonings.

Cover and simmer for 45–50 minutes, or until the pork is cooked through. Serve immediately.

Pork with Tomatoes

Serves 4

5 tablespoons olive oil

450 g/1 lb lean pork, cubed

2 garlic cloves, crushed

1 large onion, chopped

450 g/1 lb tomatoes, peeled and seeded

1 bay leaf

½ teaspoon paprika pepper

1 teaspoon salt

freshly ground black pepper

1 tablespoon freshly chopped parsley

Heat the oil in a large flameproof casserole and fry the pork, turning until browned all over. Add the garlic and onions and cook for 3–4 minutes, or until the onion has softened.

Chop the tomatoes and add to the casserole with the bay leaf, paprika pepper and salt. Bring to the boil, then cover and simmer for 30 minutes, or until the pork is cooked through.

Remove the lid and season with pepper. Stir in the parsley and serve.

Veal with Olives

Serves 4
4 tablespoons olive oil
4 garlic cloves, crushed
450 g/1 lb veal fillets
1 large onion, quartered and sliced
1 large carrot, chopped
1 celery stick, sliced
1 tablespoon flour
600 ml/1 pint/2½ cups chicken stock
juice of ½ lime
150 ml/¼ pint/ ⅔ cup sherry
1 tablespoon freshly chopped parsley
salt and freshly ground black pepper
16 green olives, pitted and quartered
lime wedges and celery leaves to garnish

Heat the oil in a flameproof casserole and fry the garlic until browned. Add the veal and fry, turning until browned all over, then remove the veal from the pan.

Add the onion, carrots and celery to the pan and cook, stirring until softened.

Add the flour and cook, stirring, for 1 minute. Remove the pan from the heat and stir in the stock, lime juice and sherry. Bring to the boil.

Return the veal to the pan, add the parsley and season the stew well. Cover and simmer for 1 hour, or until the meat is tender.

Remove the veal from the pan and transfer the sauce to a food processor or blender. Blend until smooth and heat through in the pan with the veal and olives. Serve garnished with lime wedges and celery leaves.

Beef in Cream Sauce

Serves 4

675 g/1½ lb braising or stewing steak
4 tablespoons olive oil
2 onions, halved and sliced
2 garlic cloves, crushed
1 teaspoon turmeric
1 teaspoon ground cinnamon
1 teaspoon ground cumin
pinch of ground cloves
salt and freshly ground black pepper
125 g/4 oz/¾ cup mixed no-need-to-soak dried apricots and
   dried dates, chopped
2 dried limes
1 tablespoon freshly chopped coriander (cilantro)

Remove any fat from the meat and cut the meat into cubes Heat the oil in a flameproof casserole and fry the onions and garlic for 3–4 minutes, stirring. Add the spices and cook for another 1 minute, stirring.

Stir in the meat and dried fruits. Heat the oven to 190°C/375°F/Gas 5. Place a lid on the casserole and cook in the oven for 20 minutes.

Remove the casserole from the oven and stir well. Add a little water if necessary and add the limes. Return to the oven for 10 minutes, or until the beef is cooked through. Serve with rice or couscous.

Lamb with Mint and Yogurt

Serves 4

675 g/1½ lb lean lamb, cubed

4 garlic cloves, crushed

2 onions, chopped

1 teaspoon ground allspice

1 teaspoon ground cinnamon

4 tablespoons olive oil

300 ml/½ pint/1¼ cups lamb stock

300 ml/½ pint/1¼ cups plain yogurt

1 tablespoon cornflour (cornstarch)

1 tablespoon freshly chopped mint

1 tablespoon freshly chopped coriander (cilantro)

1 tablespoon grilled (broiled) pine nuts

Heat the oven to 190°C/375°F/Gas 5. Place the meat, garlic, onion, spices and oil in a lidded casserole with the stock. Cover and cook in the oven for 20 minutes. Stir well and cook for another 20 minutes.

Mix the yogurt and cornflour in a small saucepan and heat gently, stirring until thickened. Do not allow to boil.

Add this to the lamb casserole and return to the oven for another 10 minutes. Remove from the oven and stir in the herbs. Serve immediately with rice.

Stifado

Serves 6

6 tablespoons olive oil

5 garlic cloves, chopped

4 large onions, quartered and sliced

675 g/1½ lb stewing beef, trimmed and cut into cubes

675 g/1½ lb tomatoes, seeded, peeled and quartered

3 tablespoons tomato purée

250 ml/8 fl oz/1 cup red wine

freshly ground black pepper

1 tablespoon freshly chopped marjoram

Preheat the oven to 150°C/300°F/Gas 2. Heat 4 tablespoons of the oil in a large pan and cook the garlic and onions over a gentle heat for 15 minutes, or until softened and browned. Transfer to a large casserole.

Heat the remaining oil in the pan and cook the beef until browned all over, then transfer to the casserole with the onions.

Add the tomatoes, tomato purée and wine. Season well and cover and cook in the oven for 4–5 hours, or until the meat is really tender and the sauce has become really thick. Sprinkle the marjoram over the top and serve.

Spicy Roast Beef

Serves 6

For the marinade

1 tablespoon tomato purée (paste)

1 tablespoon garlic wine vinegar

4 tablespoons olive oil

1 tablespoon soft dark brown sugar

2 garlic cloves, crushed

1 teaspoon ground ginger

juice of ½ lemon

For the meat

750 g/1¾ lb fillet of beef

2 tablespoons mixed peppercorns, crushed

1 tablespoon prepared horseradish sauce

300 ml/½ pint/1¼ cups plain yogurt

parsley leaves to garnish

Mix all the marinade ingredients together and spread over the beef fillet. Sprinkle the crushed peppercorns on top of the beef, then leave to marinate overnight.

Heat the oven to 240°C/475°F/Gas 9. Transfer the beef and juices to a roasting pan and cook in the oven for 20 minutes. Reduce the oven temperature to 220°C/425°F/Gas 7 and cook for another 25 minutes. Remove from the pan and allow to cool completely.

Stir the pan juices and horseradish sauce into the yogurt and slice the beef very thinly. Serve with salad leaves and the yogurt sauce.

Pork with Capers

Serves 4

450 g/1 lb pork fillet (tenderloin), sliced
4 tablespoons olive oil
2 garlic cloves, crushed
1 small onion, halved and sliced
125 ml/4 fl oz/½ cup red wine
juice of 1 lime
salt and freshly ground black pepper
1½ tablespoons capers
freshly chopped sage to garnish

Cook the pork in the oil in a large frying pan (skillet) until browned on all sides. Add the onion and garlic and cook for another 3 minutes, stirring.

Pour in the wine and lime juice. Season well. Simmer gently for 5–7 minutes, then increase the heat to reduce the sauce slightly. Scatter the capers and sage into the pan and mix well.

Cook for another 1–2 minutes and serve.

Liver and Onions

Serves 4

3 tablespoons freshly chopped parsley

5 tablespoons olive oil

60 g/2 oz/¼ cup butter

2 large onions, quartered and thinly sliced

2 garlic cloves, crushed

675 g/1½ lb calves' liver, thinly sliced

3–4 tablespoons beef stock (optional)

garlic croûtons to serve

Put the parsley, oil and half of the butter in a large frying pan (skillet) and cook for 1 minute. Add the onions and garlic and fry gently for 3–4 minutes, or until the onions are lightly browned. Reserve.

Melt the remaining butter in a separate pan and cook the liver for 5 minutes, adding the stock if required.

Arrange the onions on a heated plate and lay the liver on top. Scatter the croûtons on top and serve immediately.

Cassoulet

Serves 6

450 g/1 lb/2½ cups dried haricot beans, soaked overnight

6 tablespoons olive oil

2 onions, finely chopped

3 garlic cloves, crushed

1.5 litres/2¾ pints/7 cups lamb stock

1 bouquet garni

225 g/8 oz lamb fillet, cubed

350 g/12 oz pork belly, cut into six

350 g/12 oz French garlic sausage, cut into six

3 tablespoons tomato purée (paste)

1 tablespoon freshly chopped parsley

6 tablespoons fresh brown breadcrumbs

salt and freshly ground black pepper

Drain the beans, place in a large pan with clean water and bring to the boil. Boil rapidly for 10 minutes, drain and set aside.

Heat 3 tablespoons of the oil in a large pan and cook the onion and garlic until softened. Add the beans and cook for 2–3 minutes. Stir in 900 ml/1½ pints/3¾ cups of stock and bring to the boil. Add the bouquet garni and reduce the heat, then cover and simmer for 40 minutes.

Heat the oven to 180°C/350°F/Gas 4. Meanwhile, cook the meats and sausage in the remaining oil until browned and drain on paper towels.

Stir the tomato purée into the bean stew and season well. Add the parsley and remaining stock, then return the mixture to the boil and remove from the heat.

Using a draining spoon, transfer half of the beans to a deep ovenproof dish, then add the meats and top with the remaining bean mixture.

Pour the cooking liquid over the top, cover and cook in the oven for 1 hour.

Remove the cover and sprinkle the breadcrumbs over the top. Return to the oven for 45 minutes and then serve.

Souvlaki

Serves 4

675 g/1½ lb lamb fillet, cut into small cubes

16 bay leaves

4 tablespoons olive oil

3 tablespoons lemon juice

1 garlic clove, crushed

1 tablespoon freshly chopped oregano

salt and freshly ground black pepper

lemon wedges and oregano to garnish

Soak 8 small wooden skewers in water for 30 minutes. Remove from the water and thread the lamb cubes on to the skewers, placing a bay leaf at either end of the skewer.

Lay the skewers in a shallow dish. Mix the oil, lemon juice, garlic and oregano and pour over the skewers. Season and leave to marinate for 2 hours, basting occasionally.

Heat the grill (broiler) to medium and remove the skewers from the marinade. Cook the souvlaki for 10–15 minutes, turning once and basting with marinade, until cooked through. Serve with lemon wedges and oregano leaves.

Steamed Prawns with Chickpea Purée

Serves 4

120 g/4 oz/⅔ cup dried chickpeas, soaked overnight

1 litre/1¾ pints/4¼ cups fish stock

1 garlic clove

1 tablespoon rosemary leaves

teaspoon freshly chopped dill

16 large prawns (shrimps), shelled and de-veined

2 tablespoons extra-virgin olive oil

dill sprigs to garnish

Drain the chickpeas and cook in the stock with the garlic, rosemary and dill until soft. Drain, reserving half of the cooking liquid and place the reserved liquid, and the chickpeas in a food processor. Blend to a thick purée and season to taste.

Steam the prawns for 3–4 minutes, or until cooked. Spoon the chickpea purée on to serving plates and arrange four prawns on top of each serving.

Drizzle the olive oil over the top and serve garnished with dill.

White Fish in Basil Sauce

Serves 4

2 white fish fillets, skinned

juice of 2 lemons

250 ml/8 fl oz/1 cup dry vermouth

salt and freshly ground black pepper

2 tablespoons olive oil

1 litre/1¾ pints/4¼ cups fish stock

225 g/8 oz fine French green beans

1 bunch basil

1 garlic clove, crushed

3 tablespoons pine nuts

Place the fish in a shallow dish and pour half of the lemon juice and half of the vermouth over, turning the fish to coat. Season and leave to marinate for 1 hour.

Remove the fish from the marinade, reserving the marinade. Heat the oil in a frying pan (skillet) and cook the fish with the remaining vermouth for 2–3 minutes. Remove the fish and keep warm. Pour the marinade and the fish stock into the pan, bring to the boil and remove from the heat.

Cook the beans in boiling water until tender, drain and pour on the remaining lemon juice.

Place the basil, garlic and pine nuts in a food processor and blend until smooth with the fish liquid.

Spoon a little of the sauce on to serving plates and arrange the fish on top. Arrange the beans around the outside and add more sauce if required. Serve immediately.

Prawn and Courgette Layer

Serves 4

125 g/4 oz/2 cups fresh white breadcrumbs

3 tablespoons freshly grated Parmesan cheese

2 tablespoons mixed herbs, chopped

1 teaspoon cayenne pepper

2 garlic cloves, crushed

8 small courgettes (zucchini), finely sliced

24 prawns (shrimp), de-veined and cleaned

2 tablespoons olive oil

Mix the breadcrumbs, cheese, herbs, cayenne pepper and garlic together in a bowl. Lightly oil four ovenproof serving dishes and line the base of each dish with a layer of courgettes. Cover with a layer of the breadcrumb mixture and arrange 6 prawns on top of each dish.

Place another layer of breadcrumbs on each dish on top of the prawns and sprinkle half the oil.

Arrange the remaining courgettes on top of each dish, sprinkle with the remaining oil and cover with breadcrumbs. Cover each dish with kitchen foil.

Heat the oven to 200°C/400°F/Gas 6 and cook the layered bakes for 10 minutes. Serve immediately.

Swordfish with Almonds

Serves 4

1 red chilli

90 g/3 oz/¾ cup whole blanched almonds

225 g/8 oz canned plum tomatoes

1 teaspoon paprika pepper

1 garlic clove, crushed

tablespoons olive oil

2 tablespoons balsamic vinegar

4 fresh swordfish steaks

4 tablespoons passata (tomato purée)

2 tablespoons freshly chopped parsley

Seed the chilli pepper and chop finely. Toast the almonds under a grill (broiler) until golden brown. Chop the almonds very finely, almost to a paste.

Blend the tomatoes, paprika, garlic and all but 1 tablespoon of the oil. Stir in the vinegar.

Brush the fish with the remaining oil and cook under a medium grill (broiler), turning once until cooked through.

Stir the almonds and chilli into the tomato mixture and add the passata and parsley. Serve with the swordfish.

Prawn (shrimp) Skewers

Serves 4

24 uncooked large prawns (shrimp)

3 tablespoons olive oil

1 garlic clove, crushed

juice of 1 lime

1 tablespoon freshly chopped dill

salt and freshly ground black pepper

8 lime wedges

Remove the heads from the prawns, but leave the tails in place. Place the prawns in a shallow dish and mix together the oil, garlic, lime juice and dill. Season and pour over the prawns, turning to cover them. Leave to marinate for 2 hours.

Remove the prawns from the marinade and thread on to four skewers with a lime wedge at each end.

Cook under a moderately hot grill (broiler) for a few minutes, turning once, until cooked through. Serve immediately.

Monkfish with Tomato Sauce

Serves 4

4 tablespoons olive oil

I kg/2¼ lb monkfish, skinned, boned and cut into cubes

I tablespoon brandy

3 garlic cloves, crushed

I onion, chopped

2 tablespoons flour

4 tablespoons tomato purée (paste)

475 ml/16 fl oz/2 cups dry vermouth

pinch of cayenne pepper

I tablespoon freshly chopped basil

salt and freshly ground black pepper

Heat the oil over a medium heat in a large pan. Add the fish and cook quickly, browning on all sides. Pour in the brandy and heat until it ignites. Shake the pan until the flames disappear. Remove from the heat and use a draining spoon to transfer the fish to a bowl.

Add the garlic and onion to the pan and cook for 2–3 minutes, or until the onion begins to soften. Stir in the flour and cook for 1 minute.

Remove the pan from the heat and stir in the tomato purée and vermouth. Bring to the boil, stirring continuously.

Add the cayenne pepper and basil, season and simmer for 10 minutes.

Add the fish and cook for another 15 minutes, or until the fish is cooked through. Transfer to a serving dish and serve with fresh vegetables.

Trout in Vine Leaves

Serves 4

4 trout, gutted

125 ml/4 fl oz/½ cup olive oil

3 garlic cloves, crushed

1 tablespoon lemon juice

zest of 1 lemon

salt and freshly ground black pepper

2 tablespoons freshly chopped coriander (cilantro)

8 large vine leaves

lemon wedges to serve

Prick the trout all over and lay in a shallow dish. Mix the oil, garlic, lemon juice and zest, seasoning and coriander together and pour over the fish. Leave to marinate for 2 hours.

Remove the fish from the marinade and wrap each one in two vine leaves.

Cook under a moderately hot grill (broiler) for 5–10 minutes, turning once, until cooked through.

Place a fish on each serving plate and open the vine leaves. Spoon the remaining marinade over the fish and serve with lemon wedges.

Grilled King Prawns with Spicy Dip

Serves 4

750 g/1¾ lb king prawns (jumbo shrimp) in their shells

For the dip

tablespoon olive oil

2 garlic cloves, crushed

1 teaspoon ground cumin

1 teaspoon ground coriander

1 teaspoon cayenne pepper

1 red chilli, chopped

pinch of turmeric

juice of 1 lemon

Place the prawns under a moderately hot grill (broiler) and cook for 8 minutes, turning once until cooked through.

Meanwhile, whisk the dip ingredients together and pour into four small serving dishes.

Place a dish in the centre of each serving plate and arrange the prawns around it. Serve immediately.

White Fish in Spicy Sauce

Serves 4

750 g/1¾ lb white fish such as cod, skinned

5 tablespoons olive oil

2 garlic cloves, crushed

juice of 1 lime

1 teaspoon ground cumin

1 teaspoon ground coriander

½ teaspoon dill seed

1 teaspoon cayenne pepper

3 tablespoons freshly chopped coriander (cilantro)

Cut the fish into cubes and place in a shallow dish. Mix the remaining ingredients together and pour over the fish. Turn to coat the fish in the marinade and leave to marinate for 1 hour.

Transfer the fish and marinade to a pan and cook for 10 minutes, or until the fish is cooked through. Serve immediately if serving hot, or leave to cool completely and serve cold with crusty bread.

Fish Balls

Serves 4

2 slices white bread, crusts removed

675 g/1½ lb white fish fillet

2 spring onions (scallions), finely chopped

I egg

salt and freshly ground black pepper

I garlic clove

2 tablespoons freshly chopped parsley

For the sauce

I onion, chopped

4 tablespoons olive oil

I garlic clove, crushed

400 g/14 oz can tomatoes

I teaspoon cayenne pepper

I teaspoon ground coriander

I teaspoon turmeric

juice of ½ lemon

300 ml/½ pint/1¼ cups fish stock

Soak the bread in water and squeeze dry. Remove any skin and bones from the fish and mash it with a fork. Work in the remaining ingredients. Wet your hands and roll the mixture into walnut-sized balls.

To make the sauce, fry the onion in the oil for 2–3 minutes, or until browned, then add the garlic and cook for 1 minute.

Stir in the remaining ingredients and bring to the boil.

Add the fish balls to the sauce and cook for 8 minutes, or until cooked through. Serve immediately with rice or couscous.

Mussels with Pesto

Serves 4

2k g/4½ lb mussels in their shells, cleaned

125 ml/4 fl oz/½ cup dry white wine

For the pesto

60 g/2 oz/1 cup basil

2 garlic cloves

2 tablespoons pine nuts

salt and freshly ground black pepper

3 tablespoons freshly grated Parmesan cheese

5 tablespoons olive oil

2 tablespoons fine oats

Preheat the oven to 200°C/400°F/Gas 6. Place the mussels and wine in a large saucepan, then cover and cook over a high heat for 4–6 minutes, shaking the pan. Remove any unopened mussels and remove the mussels from the wine.

To make the pesto, place the basil, garlic, pine nuts, seasoning and cheese in a food processor and blend, adding the oil in a constant stream.

Spread a little pesto over each mussel and top with the oats. Place in a shallow ovenproof dish and bake in the oven for 8–10 minutes. Serve immediately, garnished with basil and lemon wedges.

Squid with Olives

Serves 4
750 g/1¾ lb medium squid
4 tablespoons olive oil
1 red onion, quartered and sliced
3 garlic cloves, chopped
400 g/14 oz can chopped tomatoes
3 celery sticks, sliced
200 ml/7 fl oz/¾ cup red wine
125 g/4 oz/1 cup stuffed green olives
celery leaves to garnish

Clean the squid and slice into rings. Heat the oven to 160°C/325°F/Gas 3.

Heat the oil in a flameproof casserole and cook the onion and garlic for 10 minutes, or until softened. Add the squid and cook for another 5 minutes.

Stir in the tomatoes, celery and wine and bring to the boil. Cover and cook in the oven for 1¼ hours, or until the squid is tender.

Remove the casserole from the oven and stir in the olives. Garnish with celery leaves and serve.

THE BAY TREE
FOOD COMPANY

Green Colossal
OLIVES
Stuffed with Garlic
290g 10oz ℮

Hot Octopus

Serves 4

450 g/1 lb prepared octopus

1 litre/1¾ pints/4¼ cups fish stock

tablespoons olive oil

juice of ½ lemon

1 onion, cut into eight

1 teaspoon mixed peppercorns

1 tablespoon freshly chopped dill

3 garlic cloves, crushed

1 teaspoon paprika

1 teaspoon cayenne pepper

1 red chilli, chopped

1 green (bell) pepper, chopped

dill and lemon wedges to serve

Plunge the prepared octopus into boiling water and cook for 5 minutes. Drain and leave to cool slightly.

Cut the octopus into 2.5 cm/1 inch pieces. Place the stock in a large saucepan, then add 2 tablespoons of the oil, the lemon juice, onion, peppercorns and dill. Bring to the boil, add the octopus, cover and simmer for 1¼ hours, or until the octopus is tender.

Drain the octopus, reserving 125 ml/4 fl oz/ ½ cup of the cooking liquid.

Heat the remaining oil in a frying pan (skillet) and add the garlic, then cook for 2 minutes, or until beginning to brown. Add the octopus, paprika, cayenne, chilli and pepper, then stir and cook for 2 minutes.

Add the reserved cooking liquid and cook, uncovered, until the sauce has reduced slightly. Serve immediately with warm bread to mop up the juices.

Aromatic Aubergines

Serves 4

2 medium aubergines (eggplants), peeled and cubed

salt

5 tablespoons olive oil

125 g/4 oz/1 cup shelled walnuts, halved

4 tablespoons vegetable stock

1 red onion, quartered and sliced

3 garlic cloves, crushed

4 tomatoes, peeled and chopped

½ teaspoon ground cinnamon

½ teaspoon ground allspice

parsley to garnish

Put the aubergines in a colander and sprinkle with salt. Leave to stand for 30 minutes, then rinse in cold water and pat dry with paper towels.

Heat the oil in a large frying pan (skillet) and cook the walnuts for 1–2 minutes, stirring. Remove from the pan with a slotted spoon. Transfer to a food processor or pestle and mortar and grind to a paste with the stock.

Reheat the oil and fry the aubergine until lightly browned. Add the onion and garlic and cook for 3–4 minutes, or until softened. Add the nut paste, the tomatoes and spices. Simmer for 15 minutes, until the aubergines are tender. Garnish and serve.

Broad Beans with Sausage

Serves 4
125 ml/4 fl oz/½ cup olive oil
6 garlic cloves, chopped
450 g/1 lb shelled broad (fava) beans
175 g/6 oz Spanish sausage, sliced and quartered
2 tablespoons freshly chopped marjoram
1 tablespoon freshly chopped mint

Heat the oil in a large pan and fry the garlic for 2 minutes, stirring until lightly browned. Add the beans and stir well to coat in the oil.

Add the sausage, then cover and cook for 20 minutes, or until the beans are tender.

Season with salt and pepper and sprinkle the herbs over the top. Serve immediately.

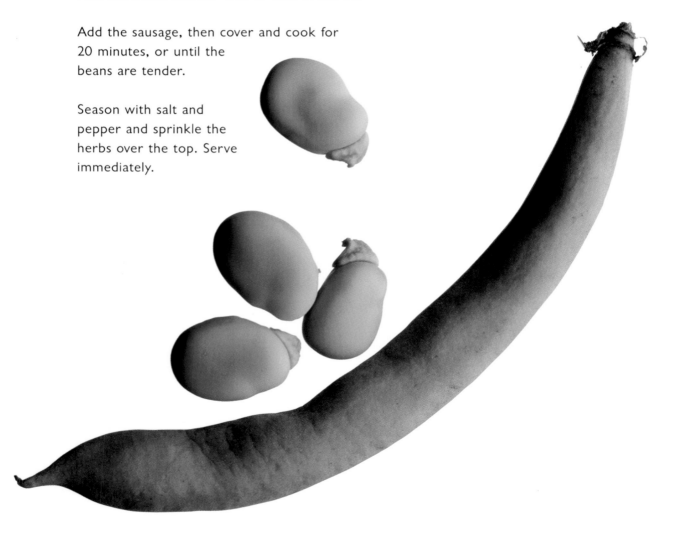

Potatoes with Onions

Serves 4

150 ml/¼ pint/⅔ cup olive oil

450 g/1 lb potatoes, cubed

2 onions, sliced

1 green (bell) pepper, chopped

1 celery stick, chopped

3 garlic cloves, crushed

1 teaspoon ground coriander

1 teaspoon cayenne pepper

6 tablespoons dry white wine

6 tablespoons vegetable stock

salt and freshly ground black pepper

1 tablespoon freshly chopped coriander (cilantro)

Heat half of the oil in a large frying pan (skillet) and add the potatoes, onions, pepper, celery and garlic, layering them into the pan. Pour on the remaining oil and cook until the potatoes begin to brown.

Mix the spices, wine and stock, then season and pour over the potatoes. Bring to the boil, then cover and simmer for 30 minutes, or until the potatoes are cooked. Sprinkle with coriander and leave to stand for 5 minutes before serving.

Tomato-stuffed Courgettes

Serves 4

4 medium courgettes (zucchini)

For the filling

1 bunch spring onions (scallions), chopped

1 red (bell) pepper, seeded and chopped

1 garlic clove, crushed

1 tablespoon freshly chopped coriander (cilantro)

1 tablespoon freshly chopped mint

? teaspoon salt

For the sauce

3 tomatoes, peeled and chopped

6 tablespoons olive oil

2 tablespoons lime juice

vegetable stock

lime wedges and salad leaves to garnish

Slice the courgettes into 3 cm/1 inch lengths. Remove some of the flesh from inside each courgette with a knife.

Mix the filling ingredients together in a small bowl and spoon into the courgettes. Arrange the courgettes in a pan.

Mix the tomatoes, oil and lime juice together and pour over the courgettes with enough stock to reach halfway up the sides of the courgettes. Bring to the boil, cover the pan and simmer for 45–60 minutes, or until the courgettes are tender.

Remove from the heat and allow to cool. Serve with lime wedges and salad leaves.

Okra in Oil

Serves 4

450 g/1 lb okra

150 ml/¼ pint/½ cup olive oil

2 onions, finely chopped

2 garlic cloves, crushed

2 teaspoon coriander seeds

1 teaspoon ground cumin

salt and freshly ground black pepper

150 ml/¼ pint/⅔ cup passata (tomato purée)

juice of 1 lemon

vegetable stock

freshly chopped parsley to garnish

Wash the okra and cut off the stems. Heat the oil in a saucepan and add the okra. Cook until lightly browned and remove from the pan with a slotted spoon.

Add the onion to the pan and cook for 5 minutes, then add the garlic, coriander, cumin and seasoning.

Stir in the passata and lemon juice and enough stock to cover the okra. Bring to the boil and then simmer for 15 minutes, stirring occasionally.

Remove from the heat and sprinkle with chopped parsley. Serve hot or cold.

Leeks in Olive Oil

Serves 4
4 large leeks
150 ml/¼ pint/⅔ cup olive oil
1 red onion, cut into eight
1 garlic clove, crushed
150 ml/¼ pint/⅔ cup vegetable stock
3 tomatoes, peeled and sliced
1 teaspoon mixed peppercorns
salt
90 g/3 oz/½ cup rice
juice of 1 lime
lime zest and marjoram to garnish

Slice the root from the leeks and cut the leeks into chunky slices. Wash well and drain.

Heat the oil in a large saucepan and add the onion, leeks and garlic. Cook for 5 minutes, stirring.

Add the stock, tomatoes, peppercorns, seasoning and rice and bring to the boil. Reduce the heat and simmer for 30 minutes, or until the rice is cooked.

Add the lime juice and sprinkle with lime zest and marjoram. Serve hot or cold.

Spinach with Olive Oil and Pine Nuts

Serves 4

450 g/1 lb spinach

4 tablespoons olive oil

3 garlic cloves, crushed

3 tomatoes, peeled and chopped

1 teaspoon salt

freshly ground black pepper

½ teaspoon ground nutmeg

1 tablespoon pine nuts

Rinse the spinach and drain well. Place in a large saucepan and cook until just limp. Drain well and squeeze out any remaining water. Chop the spinach and reserve.

Heat the oil in a large frying pan (skillet) and add the garlic. Cook for 2–3 minutes. Add the spinach and stir well. Stir in the tomatoes, salt, pepper and nutmeg, then cover and cook for 10 minutes.

Sprinkle the pine nuts over the top and serve.

Vine Leaves with Onion and Rice Stuffing

Serves 6

350 g/12 oz vine leaves

For the filling

150 ml/¼ pint/⅔ cup olive oil

1 large red onion, thinly sliced

1 red (bell) pepper seeded and thinly sliced

175 g/6 oz/1 cup white rice, washed and drained

2 tablespoons tomato purée (paste)

½ teaspoon chilli powder

1 teaspoon ground cumin

½ teaspoon ground cinnamon

30 g/1 oz/¼ cup chopped hazelnuts

1 tablespoon freshly chopped mint

For the sauce

2 tablespoons tomato purée (paste)

1.4 litres/2½ pints/6¼ cups vegetable stock

3 garlic cloves, crushed

1 chilli pepper, finely chopped

3 tablespoons lemon juice

Wash the vine leaves and place in a pan. Cover with water and cook for 15 minutes, drain well.

Heat the oil in a large saucepan and add the onions and pepper. Cook for 5 minutes, stirring. Add the rice, tomato purée and spices and cook for another 10 minutes more. Add the hazelnuts and mint and leave to cool.

Spread a vine leaf out on a chopping board, vein-side uppermost. Spoon a little of the filling across the centre and fold the leaf over the filling to encase completely.

Place the filled leaves in the base of a large saucepan, packing them in so that they remain at the base of the pan. Place a plate on top and weight it down.

Mix the sauce ingredients together and pour over the leaves. Bring to the boil, then cover and simmer for 1½–2 hours. Remove the plate from the pan and lift out the vine leaves. Arrange on serving plates and spoon the sauce around the leaves. Serve.

Broccoli and Cauliflower with Chillis

Serves 4

1 kg/2¼ lb broccoli and cauliflower, mixed

4 tablespoons olive oil

1 red chilli, sliced

4 garlic cloves, chopped

1 tablespoon lime juice

1 tablespoon freshly chopped thyme

salt and freshly ground black pepper

Cut the broccoli and cauliflower into small florets. Heat the oil in a wok or large frying pan (skillet) and add the chilli and garlic.

Stir in the broccoli and cauliflower, cover and cook over a low heat until cooked but crisp.

Stir in the lime juice and herbs, then season to taste and serve.

Baked Vegetables with Bread Crust

Serves 4

1 kg/2¼ lb mixed green vegetables, such as shredded
   cabbage, spinach, broccoli, beans and endive (chicory)

salt and freshly ground black pepper

3 slices white bread, made into crumbs

3 tablespoons olive oil

2 garlic cloves, crushed

2 tablespoons freshly grated Parmesan cheese

Cook the vegetables in boiling salted water for 3–4 minutes. Drain well and plunge into cold water. Drain and spoon into the base of a shallow ovenproof dish.

Cover the vegetables with breadcrumbs. Heat the olive oil and garlic and pour over the top. Sprinkle with Parmesan cheese and cook in a preheated oven at 200°C/400°F/Gas 6 for 10 minutes, or until the crust is golden brown. Serve immediately.

Pumpkin and Fennel with Beans

Serves 4

4 tablespoons olive oil

3 garlic cloves, crushed

450 g/1 lb pumpkin, seeded and thinly sliced

1 fennel bulb, thinly sliced

1 teaspoon cayenne pepper

1 tablespoon freshly chopped coriander (cilantro)

225 g/8 oz can white beans, drained

fennel seeds to garnish

Heat the oil in a large pan and add the garlic, then cook for 1 minute. Add the pumpkin, fennel and cayenne, then cover and cook very gently until the pumpkin is tender.

Transfer the pumpkin and fennel to a food processor and blend until smooth.

Return to the pan and add the coriander and beans. Heat through gently and serve scattered with fennel seeds.

Vegetables Baked with Eggs

Serves 4

2 aubergines (eggplants)

salt

2 large potatoes, peeled and thinly sliced

3 garlic cloves, crushed

1 red, 1 green and 1 yellow (bell) pepper,
 seeded and thinly sliced

1 courgette (zucchino), sliced

450 g/1 lb plum tomatoes, chopped

freshly ground black pepper

1 tablespoon freshly chopped parsley

4 eggs

Cut the aubergine into strips and sprinkle with salt. Leave in a colander for 30 minutes. Rinse under cold water and pat dry with paper towels.

Heat the oil in a frying pan (skillet) and cook the potatoes for 5 minutes. Add the garlic, peppers, courgette, tomatoes and aubergine, then season well and stir in the parsley.

Cook for 15–20 minutes, or until the vegetables are tender.

Break the eggs on to the surface of the vegetables and cook for 10 minutes, or until cooked through.

Creamy Garlic Potatoes

Serves 4

675 g/1½ lb potatoes
3 tablespoons olive oil
2 garlic cloves, crushed
3 tablespoons plain Greek yogurt
2 tablespoons freshly snipped chives
salt and freshly ground black pepper

Boil the potatoes in their skins for 20 minutes, or until cooked through. Drain and peel. Chop the potatoes into a bowl and add the olive oil and garlic. Mash with a potato masher or blend in a food processor.

Fold in the yogurt and chives and season well. Serve with grilled (broiled) meats.

Rocket and Parmesan Pasta

Serves 4

450 g/1 lb spaghetti

salt

For the sauce

3 tablespoons extra-virgin olive oil

2 garlic cloves, peeled

1 red chilli

125 g/4 oz/2 cups rocket (arugula) leaves

salt and freshly ground black pepper

3 tablespoons freshly grated Parmesan cheese

Cook the pasta in boiling salted water for 8–10 minutes, or until *al dente*. Drain.

Meanwhile, heat the oil for the sauce in a wok or large frying pan (skillet) and cook the garlic and chilli for 30 seconds. Remove and discard the garlic and chilli.

Add the rocket to the hot oil and stir-fry for 1–2 minutes, coating the leaves in the oil.

Pour over the drained spaghetti and toss well to mix. Season and sprinkle with the Parmesan cheese. Serve immediately.

Salmon, Bean and Olive Pasta

Serves 4

450 g/1 lb penne pasta

salt

For the sauce

6 tablespoons olive oil

1 bunch spring onions (scallions), chopped

3 garlic cloves, crushed

400 g/14 oz can plum tomatoes

2 tablespoons sun-dried tomatoes in oil, drained and chopped

1 tablespoon pitted black olives, chopped

1 teaspoon capers

225 g/8 oz salmon fillet, skinned and cubed

225 g/8 oz can cannellini beans, drained

zest of 1 lime

2 tablespoons freshly chopped coriander (cilantro)

Cook the pasta in boiling salted water for 8–10 minutes, or until *al dente* then drain well.

Meanwhile, heat the oil in a saucepan and sauté the spring onions and garlic for 2–3 minutes. Increase the heat and add the canned tomatoes and juice, breaking up the tomatoes with a spoon. Cook until the sauce thickens.

Reduce the heat, then stir in the sun-dried tomatoes, olives, capers, salmon, beans and lime zest. Season well and cook for 7–10 minutes, or until the salmon is cooked through.

Spoon the cooked pasta into serving dishes and spoon the sauce on top. Serve immediately.

Mushroom Risotto with Tomatoes

Serves 4

400 g/14 oz can chopped tomatoes

2 tablespoons tomato purée (paste)

4 tablespoons olive oil

I leek, finely chopped

2 garlic cloves, crushed

350 g/12 oz/4 cups mushrooms, roughly chopped

275 g/10 oz/2 cups Arborio rice

750 ml/1¼ pints/3 cups vegetable stock

I tablespoon freshly chopped parsley

2 teaspoons freshly chopped basil

salt and freshly ground black pepper

I–2 tablespoons freshly grated Parmesan cheese

basil leaves to garnish

Mix the tomatoes with the tomato purée in a bowl. Heat the oil in a large frying pan (skillet) and sauté the leek for 3–4 minutes, turning. Add the garlic and cook for another 30 seconds.

Add the mushrooms and stir again. Stir in the rice and cook for 2 minutes, or until the rice turns translucent. Add the tomato mixture and half of the stock. Add the herbs and season to taste.

Bring to the boil, reduce the heat and simmer gently, adding a little stock as the risotto absorbs it, for 45 minutes until the rice is creamy, or still moist and cooked through.

Sprinkle the cheese and basil over the top and serve immediately.

Chicken Couscous

Serves 4

4 tablespoons olive oil

4 chicken breast fillets, skinned and cut into chunks

2 red onions, quartered

2 carrots, cut into chunks

2 small turnips, quartered

1 courgette (zucchino), cut into chunks

1 tablespoon tomato purée (paste)

1 large tomato, seeded and cut into eight

2 garlic cloves, crushed

1 teaspoon turmeric

1 teaspoon ground coriander

1 teaspoon ground cumin

1 tablespoon clear honey

2 tablespoons no-need-to-soak dried apricots, halved

2 tablespoons raisins

salt and freshly ground black pepper

275 g/10 oz/2½ cups pre-cooked couscous

1 tablespoon pine nuts

coriander (cilantro) to garnish

Heat 1 tablespoon of the oil in a large saucepan and sauté the chicken, stirring until golden brown. Add enough water to cover the chicken and bring to the boil, skimming off any froth from the surface.

Add the onions, carrots, turnips, courgettes, tomato purée, tomato, garlic and spices, honey and fruit. Season well and simmer for 20 minutes.

Meanwhile, soak the couscous in a bowl of water for 20 minutes. Drain and place in a saucepan with 2 tablespoons of water, then heat gently, stirring often.

When the chicken and vegetables are cooked, stir the remaining olive oil into the couscous with 2 tablespoons of the stew liquid. Spoon onto a serving plate, making a well in the centre.

Spoon the chicken and vegetable stew into the centre of the couscous, sprinkle the pine nuts over the top and garnish with coriander. Serve immediately.

Pesto Sauce

Serves 4
450 g/1 lb spaghetti
salt

For the sauce
2 garlic cloves
2 large bunches basil
2 tablespoons pine nuts
4 tablespoons freshly grated Parmesan cheese
6 tablespoons olive oil
salt and freshly ground black pepper

Cook the pasta in boiling salted water for 8–10 minutes, or until *al dente*. Drain well.

Meanwhile, place the garlic, basil, pine nuts and cheese in a food processor and blend well. With the processor still running, gradually pour the oil into the sauce until well blended. Season to taste.

If liked, transfer the pesto to a saucepan and heat gently, but do not allow to boil before tossing into the spaghetti. Serve immediately.

Tagliatelle with Olive Oil and Garlic Sauce

Serves 4
450 g/1 lb tagliatelle
salt

For the sauce
garlic cloves
1 teaspoon salt
175 ml/6 fl oz/¾ cup olive oil
1 red chilli, finely chopped
freshly ground black pepper
torn basil leaves to garnish

Cook the pasta in boiling salted water for 8–10 minutes, or until *al dente*. Drain well.

Meanwhile, crush the garlic cloves and mix with the salt, or pound the garlic and salt together in a pestle and mortar. Add the olive oil to the mixture, drop by drop, blending until it reaches a smooth consistency.

Add the chilli and mix well. Heat the sauce gently in a small saucepan and toss into the pasta. Season with ground black pepper and garnish with basil. Serve immediately.

Rice with Herbs

Serves 4
225 g/8 oz/1¼ cups Arborio rice
1 tablespoon freshly chopped parsley
1 tablespoon freshly chopped mint
1 tablespoon freshly chopped oregano
1 garlic clove, crushed
2 tablespoons olive oil
freshly ground black pepper

Heat a pan of boiling water and cook the rice for 10 minutes. Drain well.

Heat the herbs, garlic and oil in a small pan and stir into the rice.

Season well with black pepper and serve immediately.

Tricolour Pasta

Serves 4

450 g/1 lb tricolour fettucine

For the sauce

8 tablespoons olive oil

30 g/1 oz/2 tablespoons butter

zest of 2 limes

salt and freshly ground black pepper

1 tablespoon freshly chopped coriander (cilantro)

1 tablespoon freshly chopped marjoram

1 tablespoon freshly chopped thyme

8 tomatoes, skinned, seeded and chopped

Parmesan cheese slivers to garnish

Cook the pasta in boiling salted water for 8–10 minutes, or until *al dente*. Drain well.

Meanwhile, heat the oil and butter in a saucepan and add the lime zest and seasoning. Stir in the herbs and chopped tomatoes and cook for 5 minutes, stirring.

Pour the sauce over the cooked pasta, tossing to mix, and serve immediately with slivers of Parmesan cheese to garnish.

Vermicelli with Nuts

Serves 4

350 g/12 oz vermicelli

salt

For the sauce

6 tablespoons olive oil

4 garlic cloves, thinly sliced

90 g/3 oz/¾ cup shelled walnuts, chopped

90 g/3 oz/¾ cup shelled hazelnuts, roughly chopped

1 tablespoon freshly chopped oregano

freshly ground black pepper

5 tablespoons freshly grated Italian cheese

oregano sprigs to garnish

Cook the pasta in boiling salted water for 8–10 minutes, or until *al dente*. Drain well.

Meanwhile, make the sauce. Heat the oil in a saucepan and add the garlic. Cook for 1 minute and then stir in the nuts and chopped oregano. Season with black pepper and add the cheese. Pour the sauce over the pasta, tossing well. Garnish with oregano sprigs and serve immediately.

Seafood Pasta

Serves 4

450 g/1 lb pasta shells

salt

For the sauce

3 tablespoons olive oil

1 red onion, chopped

1 garlic clove, crushed

½ fennel bulb, chopped

150 ml/¼ pint/⅔ cup dry vermouth

225 g/8 oz scallops

225 g/8 oz/1½ cups prawns (shrimps), shelled

freshly ground black pepper

1 tablespoon freshly chopped dill

Cook the pasta in boiling salted water for 8–10 minutes, or until *al dente*, then drain well.

Meanwhile, heat the oil in a saucepan and fry the onion, garlic and fennel for 3–4 minutes, stirring.

Heat the vermouth in a separate pan and poach the scallops for 3 minutes, then add the prawns and cook for another 3 minutes. Stir in the onion, garlic and fennel and season well.

Add the chopped herbs and spoon on to the cooked pasta. Serve immediately.

Pasta Twists with Sun-dried Tomato Sauce

Serves 4

450 g/1 lb pasta twists

salt

For the sauce

2 tablespoons freshly chopped coriander (cilantro)

5 tablespoons freshly grated Parmesan cheese

2 garlic cloves, crushed

4 tablespoons Ricotta cheese

4 tablespoons sun-dried tomatoes in oil, drained and chopped

5 tablespoons olive oil

coriander (cilantro) sprigs to garnish

Cook the pasta in boiling salted water for 8–10 minutes, or until *al dente*, then drain well.

Meanwhile, mix the coriander, Parmesan cheese, garlic, Ricotta cheese, tomatoes and olive oil, blending to make a smooth paste.

Return the pasta to a clean pan and stir in the sauce, heating gently and not boiling, until warmed through. Spoon into warm serving bowls, garnish and serve.

Red Rice

Serves 6

450 g/1 lb basmati rice

salt

pinch of turmeric

225 g/8oz/1 cup red lentils

5 tablespoons olive oil

1 leek, sliced

3 tablespoons tomato purée (paste)

1 litre/1¾ pints/4¼ cups vegetable stock

3 garlic cloves, crushed

1 teaspoon ground cumin

1 teaspoon ground coriander

1 teaspoon cumin seeds

Wash the rice and soak it in water for 1 hour. Wash the lentils and then drain both the rice and lentils well.

Heat 2 tablespoons of the oil in a saucepan and add the leek. Cook for 2–3 minutes, stirring constantly. Stir in the tomato purée, stock, salt and turmeric. Bring to the boil and add the rice and lentils. Reduce to a very low heat, cover and simmer for 30 minutes, or until the rice and lentils are cooked.

Heat the remaining oil in a separate pan and fry the garlic and spices. Add to the rice and lentils, stirring well.

Cover and steam for another 10 minutes, adding a little more stock if required. Serve immediately.

Salads

Three Pepper Salad

Serves 4

2 red (bell) peppers

2 green (bell) peppers

2 yellow (bell) peppers

For the dressing

6 tablespoons olive oil

2 tablespoons garlic wine vinegar

2 garlic cloves, crushed

1 tablespoon freshly chopped basil

½ teaspoon prepared mustard

green salad leaves and quartered cherry tomatoes

Halve the peppers and grill (broil), skin-side uppermost, until the skins begin to char and blister. Remove from the grill and place in a plastic bag. Seal and leave for 20 minutes.

Remove the peppers from the bag and peel away the skins. Seed the peppers and cut the flesh into thin strips.

Meanwhile, mix the dressing ingredients together well. Pour over the peppers, tossing to coat. Arrange a bed of salad leaves on a serving dish and pile the peppers into the centre. Garnish with cherry tomatoes and serve.

Seafood Salad with Citrus Dressing

Serves 4

125 ml/4 fl oz/½ cup dry white wine

juice of 1 lime

225 g/8 oz prepared squid, sliced

225 g/8 oz cooked, peeled, large prawns (shrimp)

60 g/2 oz/½ cup cucumber, diced

1 small yellow (bell) pepper, seeded and diced

1 tablespoon freshly chopped coriander (cilantro)

radicchio and frisée leaves to serve

For the dressing

4 tablespoons olive oil

1 tablespoon orange juice

1 tablespoon lime juice

1 tablespoon lemon juice

1 garlic clove, crushed

pinch of cayenne pepper

salt and freshly ground black pepper

Place the wine and lime juice in a saucepan with 250 ml/8 fl oz/1 cup water and bring to the boil. Add the squid and simmer for 5 minutes, or until cooked through. Drain and allow the squid to cool.

Mix the prawns and the squid together in a bowl and add the cucumber, pepper and coriander. Mix the dressing ingredients together and pour into the fish and vegetables. Toss well to coat in the dressing.

Arrange the salad leaves on a serving plate and spoon the fish mixture into the centre. Serve immediately.

Tabbouleh

Serves 4

125 g/4 oz/1 cup bulgar wheat

1 cos (romaine) lettuce

2 medium-size tomatoes, seeded and chopped

1 bunch spring onions (scallions), chopped

60 g/2 oz/½ cup cucumber, diced

1 red (bell) pepper, seeded and diced

1 bunch freshly chopped mint

1 bunch freshly chopped coriander (cilantro)

3 tablespoons olive oil

2 tablespoons lime juice

salt and freshly ground black pepper

Cover the bulgar wheat with water and leave to stand for 20 minutes, or until swollen. Drain off any water.

Arrange the lettuce leaves in a shallow serving bowl.

Mix all of the remaining ingredients together and pile into the centre of the lettuce leaves. Serve immediately.

Fennel, Chicory and Orange Salad

Serves 4

1 large fennel bulb

2 heads chicory (endive)

3 small oranges

4 tablespoons olive oil

1 tablespoon orange juice

1 tablespoon freshly chopped mint

2 tablespoons freshly chopped parsley

a few sunflower seeds, toasted

salt and freshly ground black pepper

Wash, core and thinly slice the fennel, and halve the chicory. Peel and segment the oranges. Squeeze the orange juice over the cut surface of the chicory.

Arrange the fennel and chicory on serving plates with the orange segments.

Mix all the remaining ingredients together and pour over the salad. Serve immediately.

Green Bean Salad

Serves 4
350 g/12 oz small runner beans

5 tablespoons olive oil

3 garlic cloves, crushed

1 red onion, chopped

5 canned plum tomatoes, chopped

1 teaspoon cayenne pepper

1 tablespoon freshly chopped mint

Top, tail and wash the beans and cook in boiling water for 5 minutes. Drain and refresh under cold water.

Meanwhile, heat the oil in a small saucepan and fry the garlic and onion for 3–4 minutes. Add the tomatoes and cayenne pepper, and cook for 1 minute, breaking up the tomatoes.

Add the beans and cook for another 5 minutes, then stir in the mint and remove from the heat. Transfer to a serving dish and refrigerate until completely cold before serving.

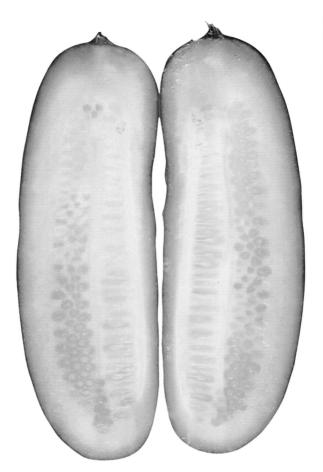

Minty Salad with Toasted Bread

Serves 4

2 pitta bread

I iceberg lettuce

125 g/4 oz/2 cups rocket (arugula)

125 g/4 oz cucumber, cut into sticks

I red onion, quartered and sliced

I bunch mint

I bunch coriander (cilantro)

2 garlic cloves, crushed

5 tablespoons olive oil

3 tablespoons lemon juice

freshly ground black pepper

Cut each pitta bread in half and cook under a low grill (broiled) until browned and crisp. Allow to cool and cut into strips.

Wash and chop the lettuce, then prepare the salad vegetables, herbs and garlic. Place in a large bowl and toss well to mix.

Whisk the olive oil and lemon juice and toss with the salad. Leave to stand for 30 minutes. Season well and toss in the bread pieces. Serve at once.

Greek Salad

Serves 4

1 green (bell) pepper), seeded and cut into rings
1 onion, thinly sliced
350 g/12 oz tomatoes, cut into thin wedges
1 cucumber, diced
125 g/4 oz feta cheese, cubed
2 tablespoons pitted black olives

For the dressing

6 tablespoons olive oil
1 garlic clove, crushed
1 tablespoon freshly chopped oregano
ground black pepper

Place the green pepper, onion, tomatoes and cucumber in a serving dish and arrange the cheese in the centre. Garnish with the olives.

Mix the dressing ingredients together and drizzle over the salad. Serve immediately.

Chickpea Salad

Serves 4

225 g/8 oz/1¼ cups chickpeas, soaked overnight

1 bunch spring onions (scallions), chopped

2 celery sticks, chopped

2 tablespoons freshly chopped coriander (cilantro)

For the dressing

1 tablespoon olive oil

2 tablespoons red wine vinegar

juice of ½ lime

1 garlic clove, crushed

salt and freshly ground black pepper

Cook the chickpeas in boiling water for 1 hour, then add some salt and cook for another 30 minutes. Drain well.

Mix the dressing ingredients and pour over the chickpeas, toss and leave to cool.

Stir in the spring onions, celery and herbs and toss to mix.

Sauces

Aioli

Makes 300 ml/½ pint/1¼ cups

2–3 garlic cloves, crushed

2 large egg yolks

250 ml/8 fl oz/1 cup olive oil

3 tablespoons lemon juice

1 tablespoon warm water

freshly ground black pepper

In a food processor or blender, blend the garlic until smooth. Add the egg yolks and blend again.

With the machine running, gradually pour the olive oil into the mixture a little at a time until the mixture begins to thicken. Stop the machine and add some lemon juice and the water.

Start the processor again and continue to add the remaining oil in a steady stream, until the mixture is fairly thick. Season with pepper. Spoon into a serving dish and serve at room temperature.

Basic Mayonnaise

Makes 600 ml/1 pint/2½ cups

1 tablespoon mustard

2 large eggs

1 teaspoon salt

2 tablespoons lemon juice

400 ml/14 fl oz/1¾ cups olive oil

In a food processor, blend the mustard, eggs and salt with the lemon juice.

With the processor still running, gradually add the olive oil, a drop at a time, until you have added about a third of the oil.

Add the remaining oil in a steady stream with the food processor still running.

Use as a base for another sauce or as a sauce on its own.

Tuna Sauce

Makes 300 ml/½ pint/1¼ cups

275 g/10 oz can tuna in oil, drained

5 anchovy fillets

1 teaspoon capers

3—4 tablespoons lime juice

1 garlic clove, crushed

150 ml/¼ pint/⅔ cup olive oil

salt and freshly ground black pepper

Blend the tuna, anchovies and capers in a food processor. Add the lime juice and garlic and mix again.

Add the oil a little at a time with the processor running until the sauce is thick. Season well and serve.

Guacamole

Makes 500 ml/17 fl oz/2¼ cups

1 hard-boiled (hard-cooked) egg, peeled

2 teaspoons mustard

125 ml/4 fl oz/½ cup olive oil

2 ripe avocado, peeled, stoned (pitted) and chopped

2 tablespoons lemon juice

1 tomato, peeled, seeded and chopped

2 tablespoons freshly chopped parsley

salt and freshly ground black pepper

Mash the hard-boiled egg and beat in the mustard. Use a fork to beat in the olive oil, a little at a time, until the mixture is thick.

Blend the avocado in a food processor with the lemon juice, and beat into the egg mixture with the tomatoes and parsley. Season and serve immediately.

Tartare Sauce

Makes 500ml/17floz/2¼ cups

250 ml/8 fl oz/1 cup basic mayonnaise (see page 138)

1 tablespoon freshly chopped tarragon

1 tablespoon freshly chopped parsley

1 tablespoon freshly chopped dill

2 tablespoons dry white wine

1 shallot, finely chopped

2 spring onions (scallions), chopped

1½ tablespoons capers, chopped

1 dill pickle or gherkin, finely chopped

freshly ground black pepper

Combine all of the ingredients well in a bowl. Cover and chill for 2–3 hours before serving.

Infusions

Use an extra-virgin olive oil for any infusions you make, as this gives a far superior flavour.

Three-quarters fill a screw-topped bottle with olive oil and add a variety of flavourings: chilli peppers for a hot oil; herbs, such as rosemary or thyme, for aromatic oils; whole peeled garlic cloves for garlic oil; sun-dried tomatoes for a tomato-flavoured oil; and peppercorns for a peppery oil.

Seal the bottles and store in a dark, cool place for at least 2 weeks before using the oils as a base for dressings and sauces, or to pour over dishes as a finishing touch.

BREADS, CAKES & PASTRIES

Onion Bread

Makes 1 loaf

225 g/8 oz/2 cups self-raising (self-rising) flour

½ teaspoon salt

300 ml/½ pint/1¼ cups water

1 teaspoon baking powder

½ teaspoon ground cumin

½ teaspoon ground coriander

pinch of chilli powder

1 teaspoon dried oregano

chopped black pitted olives

1 medium-sized onion, finely chopped

5 tablespoons olive oil

Sift the flour and salt into a large mixing bowl. Make a well in the centre and add enough water to make a firm dough. Add the baking powder, spices, herbs, olives and onion and mix well.

Knead the dough on a lightly floured surface for about 10 minutes, or until it is smooth and elastic and no longer sticky. Pour the oil into a mixing bowl and knead the dough in the oil.

Lightly grease and flour a baking sheet. Shape the dough into a loaf about 30 cm/12 inches long and cover with a clean damp tea (dish) towel. Leave to rise for 30 minutes.

Heat the oven to 180°C/350°F/Gas 4. Remove the cloth and bake the loaf for 45–50 minutes, or until it is golden brown. Remove from the baking sheet and cool before serving.

Flat Bread with Sesame Seeds

Makes 3 loaves

8 g/¼ oz/1 package dried yeast or 15 g/½ oz/1 cake fresh
(compressed) yeast
1 teaspoon sugar
300 ml/½ pint/1¼ cups warm water
1 teaspoon dried mint
4 tablespoons olive oil
450 g/1 lb/4 cups plain (all-purpose) flour
2 tablespoons sesame seeds

Dissolve the yeast and sugar in a small bowl with 4 tablespoons of the water. Leave to one side until it turns frothy and add the mint and 2 tablespoons of the oil.

Sift the flour into a mixing bowl and make a well in the centre. Pour in the yeast mixture and add enough water to make a firm dough.

Lightly flour a work surface and knead the dough for 10 minutes, or until smooth and elastic. Place in a lightly oiled bowl and cover with a clean, damp cloth. Leave in a warm place to double in size, about 2 hours.

Remove the dough from the bowl and punch down with your fist. Divide the mixture into three equal portions and shape into smooth rounds between the palms of your hands. Shape into an oval about 6 mm/¼ inch in thickness.

Using your forefinger, press four ridges into the top of each loaf. Brush the top of the loaves with the remaining oil and sprinkle the sesame seeds over the top.

Leave to rest for 30 minutes. Heat the oven to 230°C/450°F/Gas 8 and place 3 greased and floured baking sheets in the oven to heat. Remove the baking sheets and place a loaf on each. Return to the oven and cook for 15 minutes, or until golden brown. Serve warm.

Herb Bread

Makes 10 loaves

8 g/¼ oz/1 package dried yeast or 15 g/½ oz/1 cake fresh
(compressed) yeast
300 ml/½ pint/1¼ cups warm water
1 teaspoon sugar
450 g/1 lb/4 cups plain (all-purpose) flour
½ teaspoon salt

For the topping

6 tablespoons olive oil
1 teaspoon dried thyme
1 teaspoon dried oregano
1 teaspoon dried mint
2 tablespoons poppy seeds

Dissolve the yeast in 3 tablespoons of the water, stir in the sugar and leave in a warm place for 15 minutes, or until frothy.

Sift the flour into a mixing bowl with the salt and make a well in the centre. Pour in the yeast mixture and enough warm water to make a firm dough.

Knead the dough on a lightly floured surface (counter) for about 15 minutes, or until smooth and elastic. Lightly oil a mixing bowl and roll the dough in the oil. Cover with a clean, damp cloth and leave to double in size in a warm place, about 2 hours.

Divide the dough into 10 equal portions and roll each between your palms until smooth and round.

Lightly flour a board and flatten each with a rolling pin until you have a 12.5 cm/5 inch circle. Leave in a warm place to prove for 15 minutes.

Brush the tops of the loaves with a little of the oil. Mix the herbs and remaining oil together and spread over the breads. Sprinkle the poppy seeds on top. Heat the oven to 230°C/450°F/Gas 8. Place the breads on lightly oiled baking sheets and cook for 8 minutes, or until cooked through. Remove the breads from the oven and cool.

Rosemary Focaccia

Makes 2 loaves

1 teaspoon caster (superfine) sugar

1 packet easy-blend dried yeast

150 ml/¼ pint/⅔ cup warm water

2 tablespoons olive oil

450 g/1 lb/4 cups strong white bread flour

1 teaspoon salt

2 teaspoons dried rosemary

Mix the sugar and yeast together in a bowl with half of the water and leave to dissolve. Stir in the olive oil.

Sift the flour and salt into a mixing bowl and add the rosemary. Make a well in the centre and pour in the yeast mixture. Mix to a dough and turn onto a lightly floured board.

Knead the dough until smooth and elastic, about 10 minutes, then place in a lightly oiled bowl. Cover with a clean damp cloth and leave in a warm place to rise for 2 hours.

Remove the dough from the bowl and knead again for 2 minutes. Divide in half and shape each piece of dough into a thick round, about 20 cm/8 inches in diameter.

Brush the top of the loaves with olive oil and bake in a preheated oven, 200°C/400°F/Gas 6 for 30 minutes, or until cooked through. Remove from the oven and cool on a wire rack before serving.

Dough Balls

Makes 48

1 teaspoon caster sugar

1 packet easy-blend dried yeast

150 ml/¼ pint/⅔ cup warm water

2 tablespoons olive oil

450 g/1 lb/4 cups strong white bread flour

1 teaspoon salt

oil for greasing

Mix the sugar and yeast with half of the water. Leave to stand in a warm place for 10 minutes, or until dissolved. Stir in the olive oil.

Sift the flour and salt into a mixing bowl and make a well in the centre. Pour in the yeast and mix to a dough, adding extra water as required.

Turn the dough on to a floured work surface and knead for 10 minutes. Return the dough to a lightly oiled bowl. Cover with a clean damp cloth and leave in a warm place to rise for 2 hours.

Remove from the bowl and knead for 2 minutes. Break off small pieces of dough, the size of marbles, and place on a greased sheet.

Heat the oven to 220°C/425°F/Gas 7 and cook the balls for 7–8 minutes, or until golden brown. Remove and allow to cool. To serve warm, heat the balls under a hot grill (broiler) for 30 seconds.

Italian Bread

Makes 4 loaves

? teaspoon caster (superfine) sugar

1 tablespoon easy-blend dried yeast

500 ml/17 fl oz/2¼ cups warm water

3 tablespoons olive oil

675 g/1½ lb/6 cups strong white bread flour

2 teaspoons salt

2 tablespoons grated Parmesan cheese

Mix the sugar and yeast with 150 ml/¼ pint/ ⅔ cup of the water and leave in a warm place until dissolved. Add the olive oil and the remaining water.

Sift the flour and salt into a mixing bowl, add the cheese and make a well in the centre. Add the yeast mixture to the flour and mix to a dough.

Turn out on to a floured board, cover with a clean damp cloth and leave for 5 minutes. Knead the dough for 10 minutes and return to a lightly oiled bowl. Cover and leave to rise again for 2 hours.

Knead the dough for 5 minutes and divide into four equal portions. Shape each into a flat oblong and leave for 15 minutes.

Heat the oven to 200°C/400°F/Gas 6 and cook the loaves on baking sheets for 15 minutes, or until cooked through.

Saffron Bread

Makes 1 loaf

450 g/1 lb/4 cups strong white bread flour

1 teaspoon salt

1 teaspoon freshly chopped sage

large pinch of saffron strands

1 teaspoon turmeric

1 tablespoon fresh yeast

1 teaspoon caster (superfine) sugar

3 tablespoons olive oil

Blend the flour, salt and sage in a bowl. Place the saffron in 2 tablespoons hot water, add the turmeric and leave to stand. Blend the yeast, sugar and 125 ml/4 fl oz/½ cup of water and allow to stand for 10 minutes, or until frothy.

Add the yeast, saffron water and olive oil to the flour and mix to a dough. Knead on a floured surface (counter) for 2 minutes, then cover with a clean damp cloth and leave to stand in a warm place for 1 hour.

Turn the dough on to a floured surface (counter) and knead for 2 minutes. Oil a standard 450 g/1 lb loaf tin and press the dough into the tin (pan). Cover and leave to prove for 30 minutes.

Heat the oven to 200°C/400°F/Gas 6 and cook the bread for 30 minutes, or until risen and golden. Turn out on to a wire rack to cool before serving.

Garlic and Herb Italian Bread

Makes 4 loaves

½ teaspoon caster (superfine) sugar

1 tablespoon easy-blend dried yeast

500 ml/17 fl oz/2¼ cups warm water

3 tablespoons olive oil

2 garlic cloves, crushed

1 tablespoon freshly chopped marjoram

675 g/1½ lb/6 cups strong white bread flour

2 teaspoons salt

olive oil, salt and cayenne pepper for topping

Mix the sugar and yeast in a bowl with 150 ml/¼ pint/⅔ cup of the water and leave until dissolved. Add the olive oil, garlic and marjoram.

Sift the flour and salt into a mixing bowl and make a well in the centre. Pour in the yeast mixture and the remaining water and mix to a smooth dough.

Turn the dough on to a floured board and leave for 5 minutes. Knead the dough for 10 minutes and return to a lightly oiled bowl. Cover with a clean damp cloth and leave in a warm place to rise for 2 hours.

Knead the dough again and divide into four equal pieces. Shape into long flat loaves, cover and stand for 10 minutes.

Heat the oven to 200°C/400°F/Gas 6. Brush the top of the loaves with oil, sprinkle with salt and cayenne and cook on baking sheets for 12–15 minutes, or until cooked through. Allow to cool on wire racks before serving.

Spanish Magdalenas

Serves 4

225 g/8 oz/1 cup caster (superfine) sugar

5 tablespoons olive oil

3 eggs

6 egg whites

450 g/1 lb/4 cups plain (all-purpose) flour

Heat the oven to 200°C/400°F/Gas 6. Beat the sugar and oil together then beat in the whole eggs. Whisk the egg whites until stiff and peaking, then fold them into the mixture.

Gradually fold in the flour to give a dropping consistency.

Spoon the mixture on to greased baking sheets, making small rounds and spacing them apart. Bake for 12 minutes, or until golden brown. Cool before serving.

Churros

Serves 4
300 ml/½ pint/1¼ cups water
3 tablespoons olive oil
½ teaspoon salt
200 g/7 oz/1¾ plain (all-purpose) flour
oil for deep-frying
caster (superfine) sugar
225 g/8 oz/8 squares plain (semi-sweet) chocolate

Put the water, oil and salt in a large saucepan and bring to the boil. Remove from the heat and add the flour, beating well until the mixture forms a dough and comes away from the sides of the pan.

Heat the oil for deep-frying to 170°C/340°C. Place the mixture in a piping bag fitted with a star nozzle (tips) and pipe 10 cm/4 inch lengths of dough into the hot oil. Fry a few at a time until golden brown. Remove from the oil with a slotted draining spoon and drain on paper towels.

Continue until all the dough has been used. Sprinkle the hot churros with caster sugar.

Melt the chocolate in a bowl over a pan of hot water and transfer to a serving dish. Serve with the churros.

Citrus Doughnuts

Serves 4

350 g/12 oz/1½ cups caster (superfine) sugar

150 ml/¼ pint/⅔ cup olive oil

150 ml/¼ pint/⅔ cup orange juice, lemon juice and
   lime juice, mixed

grated zest of 1 lime

1 teaspoon ground cinnamon

½ teaspoon allspice

750 g/1¾ lb/7 cups plain (all-purpose) flour

2 eggs, separated

2 teaspoons bicarbonate of soda (baking soda)

oil for deep-frying

Mix 125 g/4 oz/½ cup of the caster sugar, the
oil, the fruit juices, lime zest, cinnamon and
allspice. Add half of the flour, the egg yolks
and bicarbonate of soda.

Beat the egg whites until stiff and peaking and
gently fold into the mixture. Gradually fold in
the remaining flour until the dough is firm.

Roll the dough into a long sausage shape and
cut off 3 cm/1½ inch pieces. Shape each of
these into rings.

Heat the oil for deep frying to 170°C/340°C
and fry the doughnuts a few at a time until they
puff up and are golden brown. Remove with a
slotted draining spoon and drain on paper
towels. Repeat until all of the dough is cooked.

Sprinkle the doughnuts with the remaining
sugar and serve.

Carrot Cake

Serves 12

225 g/8 oz/12 cups self-raising (self-rising) flour

1 teaspoon baking powder

150 g/5 oz/⅓ cup Demerara sugar

1 teaspoon ground cinnamon

60 g/2 oz/½ cup shelled pecan nuts, chopped

60 g/2 oz/½ cup sultanas (golden raisins)

125 g/4 oz/1 cup carrots, grated

2 ripe bananas, mashed

2 eggs

150 ml/¼ pint/⅔ cup olive oil

4 tablespoons plain yogurt

90 g/3 oz/⅓ cup cream cheese

60 g/2 oz/⅓ cup icing (confectioner's) sugar, sifted

pecan nuts and ground cinnamon to decorate

Heat the oven to 180°C/350°F/Gas 4. Grease and base line a 20 cm/8 inch deep round cake tin (pan). Sift the flour and baking powder together into a large mixing bowl and stir in the sugar and cinnamon. Add the nuts, sultanas, carrots and bananas, mixing well. Add the eggs and oil and beat well to mix thoroughly.

Spoon the mixture into the prepared tin and bake for 1 ? hours, or until a skewer inserted in the centre comes out clean. Remove from the tin and allow the cake to cool completely on a wire rack.

Meanwhile, place the yogurt in a mixing bowl with the cheese and icing sugar and beat until soft and creamy. Spread on top of the cake and decorate. Serve immediately or store in the refrigerator.